Practical Guide For The
CHILD BEHAVIOR CHECKLIST

And
RELATED MATERIALS

Stephanie H. McConaughy & Thomas M. Achenbach
Department of Psychiatry
University of Vermont

Request for Research and Clinical Papers

The authors would appreciate receiving reports of research and clinical use of the Child Behavior Checklist and related instruments. Please include author's name, address, and telephone number, as well as all available bibliographic information. Information on ordering this *Guide* and other CBCL materials can be obtained from:

Thomas M. Achenbach
Department of Psychiatry
University of Vermont
Burlington, VT 05401

Proper bibliographic citation for this *Guide*:

McConaughy, S.H., & Achenbach, T.M. (1988). *Practical guide for the Child Behavior Checklist and related materials.* Burlington, VT: University of Vermont Department of Psychiatry.

Related Books

Achenbach, T.M. (1985). *Assessment and taxonomy of child and adolescent psychopathology.* Newbury Park, CA: Sage Publications.

Achenbach, T.M., & Edelbrock, C. (1983). *Manual for the Child Behavior Checklist and Revised Child Behavior Profile.* Burlington, VT: University of Vermont Department of Psychiatry.

Achenbach, T.M., & Edelbrock, C. (1986). *Manual for the Teacher's Report Form and Teacher Version of the Child Behavior Profile.* Burlington, VT: University of Vermont Department of Psychiatry.

Achenbach, T.M., & Edelbrock, C. (1987). *Manual for the Youth Self-Report and Profile.* Burlington, VT: University of Vermont Department of Psychiatry.

Achenbach, T.M., & McConaughy, S.H. (1987). *Empirically-based assessment of child and adolescent psychopathology: Practical applications.* Newbury Park, CA: Sage Publications.

Library of Congress #: 87-73078   ISBN 0-938565-03-6

Printed in the United States of America   10 9 8 7 6 5 4 3 2

Note: Some small changes were made in the 11-88 editions of the CBCL, TRF, and YSR, but these do not affect scoring.

PREFACE

As we developed the Child Behavior Checklist for Ages 2-3 and for Ages 4-16, the Teacher's Report Form, the Youth Self-Report, and the Direct Observation Form, we have published reliability, validity, and standardization data, as well as the basic procedures for using these instruments. We have also published books on the conceptual background and on applications of our procedures to a variety of cases. In view of the growing body of information spread across numerous publications, we thought it would be helpful to provide a practical, nontechnical overview of the essential features of each instrument and the important differences among the instruments.

This *Guide* serves as an introduction to all the instruments for those who are unfamiliar with them and as a quick reference to essential information for those who are already familiar with them. It also highlights relations among the instruments and illustrates case reports integrating a variety of assessment data from multiple sources. The Reader's Guide following this Preface provides an overview of the contents to aid users in quickly locating pertinent material.

We are grateful to Judy Ewell and Kathleen Talbert for their careful work in preparing this *Guide* and to Craig Edelbrock, Elizabeth Flannery, John Helminski, David Jacobowitz, Howard Knoff, Pam Langelier, and Mimi Pantuhova for their critiques of the manuscript. We are also grateful to the W. T. Grant Foundation and the Spencer Foundation for their support of important portions of the research on which this *Guide* is based.

iii

READER'S GUIDE

I. Introductory material needed by most readers

    A. Introduction to the Guide ....Chapter 1
    B. Multiaxial empirically-based assessment .Chapter 2

II. Overview of each instrument

    A. Child Behavior Checklist for Ages 4-16 ..Chapter 3
    B. Child Behavior Checklist for Ages 2-3 ...Chapter 4
    C. Teacher's Report Form ....Chapter 5
    D. Youth Self-Report ....Chapter 6
    E. Direct Observation Form ....Chapter 7

III. Illustrative reports of multiaxial empirically-based assessment

    A. Clinical assessment ....Chapter 8
    B. Forensic assessment..................Chapter 9

IV. Answers to commonly asked questions ....Chapter 10

CONTENTS

Preface iii
Reader's Guide iv
List of Figures viii
List of Tables x

1. Introduction 1
   Plan of this Guide 3

2. Multiaxial Empirically-Based Assessment 4
   Features of Multiaxial Empirically-Based Assessment 7
      Empirically-Derived Syndromes 7
      Systematic Organization 7
      Multiple Informants 8
      Comprehensive Assessment 8
      Normative Data 8
      Efficient and Economical 9
   Summary 11

3. The Child Behavior Checklist for Ages 4-16
   (CBCL/4-16) 12
   Scores and Scales of the CBCL/4-16 12
      Competence Scales 18
      Problem Scales 21
      Summary of Cutoff Scores 27
   Multiaxial Empirically-Based Assessment Initiated
   with the CBCL 28
   Summary 32

4. The Child Behavior Checklist for Ages 2-3
   (CBCL/2-3) 33
   Scores and Scales of the CBCL/2-3 33
      Problem Scales 36
      Summary of Cutoffs 39
   Summary 39

5. **The Teacher's Report Form (TRF)** 40
   Scores and Scales of the TRF 40
      Adaptive Functioning Scales 45
      Problem Scales 45
      Summary of Cutoffs 50
   Multiaxial Empirically-Based Assessment Initiated
      with the TRF 50
   Summary 56

6. **The Youth Self-Report (YSR)** 57
   Scores and Scales of the YSR 57
      Competence Scales 62
      Problem Scales 64
      Summary of Cutoffs 66
   Multiaxial Empirically-Based Assessment Initiated
      with the YSR 67
   Summary 69

7. **The Direct Observation Form (DOF)** 71
   Training and Use 71
   Scores and Scales of the DOF 74
      On-Task, Internalizing, Externalizing, and Total
         Problem Scales 75
      Narrow-Band Scales 75
      Summary of Cutoffs and Mean Scores 79
   Summary 80

8. **Reporting Results of Multiaxial Empirically-
   Based Assessment** 82
   Example 1: A Comprehensive Evaluation Report .. 83
   Evaluation Report 84
   Example 2: Summary Report of an Evaluation 98
   Summary of Evaluation 99
   Example 3: Summary Report for School 102
   Summary of Evaluation 103
   Summary 109

9. **Forensic Reports Involving Empirically-Based
    Assessment** 110
    Example: A Child Forensic Evaluation 111
    Child Evaluation Report 111
    Summary 128

10. **Answers to Commonly Asked Questions** 129
    General Questions 129
    Comparisons between Instruments 134

References 139

Index 142

List of Figures

3-1. Social competence items of the Child Behavior
Checklist for Ages 4-16 13
3-2. Problem items of the Child Behavior Checklist
for Ages 4-16 15
3-3. Hand-scored version of the CBCL/4-16 competence
scales for 11-year-old Michael 19
3-4. Computer-scored version of the CBCL/4-16
competence scales for 11-year-old Michael 22
3-5. Hand-scored version of the CBCL/4-16 problem
scales for 11-year-old Michael 23
3-6. Computer-scored version of the CBCL/4-16 problem
scales for 11-year-old Michael 26
3-7. Illustrative sequence of empirically-based assessment where the parent is the first informant 29
4-1. The Child Behavior Checklist for Ages 2-3 34
4-2. Hand-scored version of CBCL/2-3 profile for
3-year-old Bobby 38
5-1. Pages 1 and 2 of the Teacher's Report Form 41
5-2. Pages 3 and 4 of the Teacher's Report Form 43
5-3. Hand-scored version of TRF adaptive functioning
scales for 11-year-old Michael 47
5-4. Hand-scored version of the TRF problem scales
for 11-year-old Michael 49
5-5. Illustrative sequence of empirically-based assessment where the teacher is the first informant 52
6-1. Competence items of the Youth Self-Report 58
6-2. Problem items of the Youth Self-Report 60
6-3. Hand-scored version of the YSR competence scales
for 11-year-old Michael 63
6-4. Hand-scored version of the YSR problem scales
for 11-year-old Michael 65
6-5. Illustrative sequence of empirically-based assessment where an adolescent is the first informant 68
7-1. Items of the Direct Observation Form 72

7-2. Computer-scored version of the DOF on-task and broad-band scale scores for 11-year-old Michael ... 76

7-3. Computer-scored version of the DOF narrow-band scale scores for 11-year-old Michael 78

9-1. Computer-scored version of the CBCL/4-16 problem scales for mother's ratings of 4-year-old Stephen 117

9-2. Computer-scored version of the CBCL/4-16 problem scales for father's ratings of 4-year-old Stephen 119

9-3. Computer-scored version of the CBCL/2-3 problem scales for mother's ratings of 3-year-old Melanie . 124

9-4. Computer-scored version of the CBCL/2-3 problem scales for father's ratings of 3-year-old Melanie .. 125

List of Tables

2-1. Examples of Multiaxial Materials 5

2-2. The Child Behavior Checklist and Related Materials 6

2-3. General Features of the CBCL and Related Instruments 10

3-1. Scales Scored from the Child Behavior Checklist for Ages 4-16 17

3-2. Explanations of Scores on the Competence Scales of the Child Behavior Profile 20

3-3. Explanations of Scores on the Problem Scales of the Child Behavior Profile 24

3-4. Explanations of Additional Scores on the Problem Scales of the Computer-Scored Child Behavior Profile 25

3-5. Clinical Cutoff Points for CBCL/4-16 Scales 27

4-1. Scales Scored from the Child Behavior Checklist for Ages 2-3 36

4-2. Means and Standard Deviations for CBCL/2-3 Scales 37

4-3. Clinical Cutoff Points for CBCL/2-3 Scales 39

5-1. Scales Scored from the Teacher's Report Form 46

5-2. Explanations of Scores on the Adaptive Functioning Scales of the TRF Profile 48

5-3. Clinical Cutoff Points for TRF Scales 51

6-1. Scales Scored from the Youth Self-Report 62

6-2. Clinical Cutoff Points for YSR Scales 66

7-1. Scales Scored from the Direct Observation Form .. 74

7-2. Explanations of Scores on the On-Task and Broad-Band Problem Scales of the DOF Profile ... 77

7-3. Explanations of Scores on the Narrow-Band Scales of the DOF Profile 79

7-4. Summary of Cutoffs and Mean Scores for DOF Scales 80

Chapter 1
Introduction

Five forms of the Child Behavior Checklist have been developed to fill a variety of needs. The most basic need is to describe children's competencies and problems as they are seen by parents, teachers, observers, and children themselves. This is essential for obtaining a picture of the child's functioning from various important perspectives. The forms can be readily used in diverse contexts, including mental health services, schools, medical settings, forensic evaluations, residential treatment centers, and research. The five forms are the Child Behavior Checklist for Ages 4-16 (CBCL/4-16), Child Behavior Checklist for Ages 2-3 (CBCL/2-3), Teacher's Report Form (TRF), Youth Self-Report (YSR), and Direct Observation Form (DOF).

Beside providing descriptions of specific competencies and problems, the forms are scored on profile scales that compare a child with normative samples of peers in terms of particular types of competencies and syndromes of problems. Quantitative scale scores and total scores enable users to identify degrees of deviance in particular areas as reported by a particular informant, to compare the amount of deviance indicated in reports by different informants, and to measure changes in functioning from assessment at one point in time to another. The scoring profiles are also designed to reveal patterns that characterize children's functioning in a more comprehensive manner than scores on single scales taken one-by-one.

As we have developed each rating form, we have published research findings and technical data (e. g., Achenbach & Edelbrock, 1981, 1983, 1986, 1987; Achenbach, Edelbrock, & Howell, 1987; McConaughy, Achenbach, & Gent, 1988; Reed & Edelbrock, 1983). We have also published books and articles

1

detailing the conceptual background (Achenbach, 1985) and practical applications to a variety of cases (Achenbach & McConaughy, 1987; McConaughy, 1985; McConaughy & Achenbach, 1988). This book differs from those more specialized publications in providing a convenient summary of the five forms of the Child Behavior Checklist. It also provides illustrative evaluation reports that demonstrate how to combine findings from these instruments with findings from other assessment procedures for communication with different consumers.

Although some readers may not seek much more information than presented in this book, the *Manuals* for the CBCL, TRF, and YSR contain extensive information on the empirical basis for the instruments, their psychometric properties, relations to other instruments, applications in various contexts, and answers to common questions about each instrument. Our book of case illustrations (Achenbach & McConaughy, 1987) presents a variety of CBCL, TRF, YSR, and DOF findings. It also provides guidelines for relating our instruments to the diagnostic categories of the American Psychiatric Association's (1987) *Diagnostic and Statistical Manual* (DSM) and the special education categories of Public Law 94-142, the Education of the Handicapped Act (1977, 1981). Those who use the instruments are advised to be familiar with the more detailed presentations in the *Manuals*.

This *Guide* supplements the more detailed presentations needed by users of each instrument in the following ways:

1. For those who are not familiar with any of the instruments, it provides an introduction to what they are and how they are used.

2. For users who are familiar with one or more of the instruments, it shows how each instrument relates to the others.

3. It provides a quick reference to the most important aspects of our multiaxial assessment model, scales and scores for each instrument, the relations among

the instruments, and formats for incorporating findings into evaluation reports.

We have written this *Guide* now, because we have completed the basic set of instruments for obtaining data from parents, teachers, adolescents, and observers of children's behavior in group settings such as school. We will soon complete a semi-structured clinical interview and related assessment instruments that will add a new facet to our empirically-based assessment procedures. Because proper use of the interview requires training and experience on the part of interviewers, it does not lend itself readily to the quick-reference format of this *Guide*. However, future publications on the interview will include information on its relations to the forms descibed here.

PLAN OF THIS GUIDE

Chapter 2 presents our multiaxial assessment model, the instruments designed for each axis, and the general characteristics of each instrument. Chapters 3 through 7 present details of the Child Behavior Checklist for Ages 4-16 (CBCL/4-16), Child Behavior Checklist for Ages 2-3 (CBCL/2-3), Teacher's Report Form (TRF), Youth Self-Report (YSR), and Direct Observation Form (DOF). We discuss the CBCL/4-16 first because it is the original form upon which all other forms are based. Chapter 8 provides examples of clinical evaluation reports, including a detailed presentation of findings in a comprehensive report, a summary report for communicating to other practitioners, and a summary report for teachers and other school staff emphasizing recommendations for educational programming. Chapter 9 illustrates applications of our materials to a forensic case, including a portion of a forensic report. To provide a quick reference to overarching questions, Chapter 10 addresses commonly asked questions that cut across the different instruments. Questions regarding individual instruments are answered in the Commonly Asked Questions chapter of each *Manual*.

Chapter 2
Multiaxial Empirically-Based Assessment

To take account of the multifaceted nature of children's problems, we have proposed a model called *multiaxial empirically-based assessment* (Achenbach, 1985; Achenbach & McConaughy, 1987; McConaughy & Achenbach, 1988). This model emphasizes that assessment should utilize standardized procedures to identify strengths and weaknesses in a variety of areas based on data from multiple sources. Because children's functioning often varies from one area or situation to another and there can be multiple causes for problems, the goal is to use what each procedure reveals about needs for help in different contexts. In some cases, multiaxial assessment may reveal that certain interaction partners, such as a parent or teacher, need changing more than the child does. In other cases, multiaxial assessment may show that one type of intervention is needed for one context but a different type is needed for another context.

Table 2-1 outlines our model in terms of five assessment axes applicable from preschool through high school: *I. Parent Reports, II. Teacher Reports, III. Cognitive Assessment, IV. Physical Assessment*, and *V. Direct Assessment of the Child.* Procedures are listed for obtaining standardized data, as well as relevant history and other important information not addressed through standardized assessment. Axes III and IV list procedures for obtaining information on children's cognitive functioning, school achievement, physical development, and medical needs. Axes I, II, and V include measures we have developed for assessing children's social competencies and behavioral/emotional problems: the Child Behavior Checklist

Table 2-1
Examples of Multiaxial Assessment

Age Range	Axis I Parent Reports	Axis II Teacher Reports	Axis III Cognitive Assessment	Axis IV Physical Assessment	Axis V Direct Assessment of Child
2-5	CBCL/2-3 CBCL/4-16 History Parent interview	Preschool records Teacher interview	Ability tests Perceptual-motor tests Language tests	Height, weight Medical exam Neurological exam	Observation during play Interview
6-11	CBCL/4-16 History Parent interview	TRF School records Teacher interview	Ability tests Achievement tests Perceptual-motor tests Language tests	Height, weight Medical exam Neurological exam	DOF Semi-structured clinical interview
12-18	CBCL/4-16 History Parent interview	TRF School records Teacher interview	Ability tests Achievement tests Language tests	Height, weight Medical exam Neurological exam	DOF YSR Clinical interview Self-concept measures Personality tests

(CBCL/2-3 and CBCL/4-16), Teacher's Report Form (TRF), Direct Observation Form (DOF), and Youth Self-Report (YSR).

The five versions of the Child Behavior Checklist constitute a family of standardized, empirically-based instruments for obtaining data from multiple informants, including parents, teachers, observers, and the children themselves. As indicated in Chapter 1, details of the development, reliability, validity, and applications of the instruments are presented in separate *Manuals* by Achenbach and Edelbrock for the CBCL (1983), TRF (1986), and YSR (1987). Table 2-2 summarizes the materials currently available for these empirically-based procedures. Hand-scored and computer-scored profiles are available for all five instruments. We will present examples of both the hand- and computer-scored profiles for the CBCL/4-16 in Chapter 3, but will present only one version for instruments discussed in subsequent chapters.

Table 2-2
The Child Behavior Checklist and Related Materials

Instruments
Child Behavior Checklist (CBCL/2-3)
Child Behavior Checklist (CBCL/4-16)
Teacher's Report Form (TRF)
Youth Self-Report (YSR)
Direct Observation Form (DOF)

Additional Materials
Manual for CBCL/4-16 and Revised Child Behavior Profile
Manual for TRF and Teacher Profile
Manual for YSR and Youth Profile
Computer Scoring Programs (Apple II, IIc, IIe, II+, IBM-PC, and IBM-PC compatibles)

FEATURES OF MULTIAXIAL EMPIRICALLY-BASED ASSESSMENT

Before proceeding to more detailed descriptions of each instrument in subsequent chapters, we will discuss the general features of our approach.

Empirically-Derived Syndromes

The first feature concerns the empirical derivation of syndrome scales. All five instruments are scored on scales consisting of syndromes of behavioral/emotional problems that were found to co-occur in factor analyses of informants' ratings of large samples of children. That is, rather than making a priori assumptions about which items should comprise each scale, we used empirical procedures to identify the problems that actually occur together to form syndromes. This avoids restricting assessment to assumed diagnostic categories that may in fact lack empirical support.

Systematic Organization

A second feature is the aggregation of problems and competencies into profiles. All the scoring profiles have two levels of problem scales: (1) *narrow-band scales* consisting of syndromes derived from factor analyses of individual items; and (2) *broad-band scales* derived from second-order factor analyses of the narrow-band scales to produce groupings designated as Internalizing and Externalizing problems. The organization into narrow-band and broad-band scales facilitates evaluation of children's problems at relatively differentiated and more global levels. Competencies are also grouped into scales on the various instruments. This approach enables the practitioner to organize information in a systematic and useful way. It is then possible to focus attention on syndromes of items found to co-occur rather than dealing with separate problems one-by-one.

Multiple Informants

A third feature is the use of multiple sources of data, including parents, teachers, direct observers, and self-reports by adolescents. The instruments designed for each type of informant were factor analyzed separately, producing syndrome scales that vary somewhat from one instrument to another. The variations between the syndrome scales obtained from different instruments reflect variations in the patterning and prevalence of problems as seen by different informants, as well as some variations in the instruments themselves. Nevertheless, certain syndromes, such as those designated as Aggressive and Depressed, had counterparts in ratings on all five instruments. A Delinquent syndrome was found in CBCL/4-16, TRF, and YSR ratings, but not in CBCL/2-3 or DOF ratings. Other syndromes varied more across the five instruments, reflecting greater situational specificity.

Comprehensive Assessment

A fourth feature is the comprehensiveness of assessment. The diverse items on the five instruments enable the practitioner to obtain information on a broad range of potential problems rather than focusing only on the referral complaints or problems that seem most salient at the time. The use of multiple instruments also makes it possible to examine differences in problems reported by different informants.

Normative Data

A fifth feature concerns the normative data available for the profile scales of the five instruments. Separate norms have been constructed for each instrument. Standard scores (normalized *T* scores) and percentiles show how a child compares with normative samples of the same sex and age range on each scale of the relevant profile of the CBCL/2-3, CBCL/4-16, TRF, and YSR. The DOF provides *T* scores and percentile cutoffs for the total problem score. However, because of the limited variance in scores, only raw scores and percentile cutoffs are computed for the DOF narrow-band scales and for the Internalizing and Externalizing scores.

The normative data enable the evaluator to judge the degree of deviance in reported behavior in relation to what is reported for randomly selected nonreferred children. It is then possible to identify areas in which the reports indicate functioning in the normal versus clinical range. The profiles of scales highlight strengths and problems, just as high and low subtest scores on intelligence tests highlight patterns of cognitive functioning. A broken line on each scoring profile indicates cutoff points between the normal and clinical range.

Efficient and Economical

A final feature is the efficiency and low cost of the empirically-based procedures. The CBCL, TRF, and YSR can be self-administered in about 15 minutes. The DOF can be scored by school observers on the basis of 10-minute observation periods. Clerical workers can hand score profiles in about 10-15 minutes or score them on microcomputers in 3-5 minutes. These procedures are much less costly than psychological testing or clinical interviewing. By having the checklists completed at intake, practitioners can use face-to-face client contacts more efficiently to follow up on the main problems revealed by the profiles. The empirically-based procedures are not intended to replace other forms of assessment, but to make assessment more focused and cost-effective. Table 2-3 summarizes the general features of the five versions of the CBCL, including the informant, subject group covered, and the types of scales derived from each instrument. Chapters 3 through 7 detail each instrument's specific features, scores, and scales.

Table 2-3
General Features of the CBCL and Related Instruments

Instrument	Informant	Standardization Group	Scales
Child Behavior Checklist/2-3 (CBCL/2-3; blue form)	Parent	Boys/Girls 2-3	Total Problems Internalizing Externalizing Syndromes
Child Behavior Checklist/4-16 (CBCL/4-16; blue form)	Parent	Boys 4-5 Girls 4-5 Boys 6-11 Girls 6-11 Boys 12-16 Girls 12-16	Total Competence Activities Social School Total Problems Internalizing Externalizing Syndromes
Teacher's Report Form (TRF; green form)	Teacher	Boys 6-11 Girls 6-11 Boys 12-16 Girls 12-16	School Performance Adaptive Functioning Total Problems Internalizing Externalizing Syndromes
Youth Self-Report (YSR; buff form)	Youth	Boys 11-18 Girls 11-18	Total Competence Activities Social Total Problems Internalizing Externalizing Syndromes
Direct Observation Form (DOF; yellow form)	Observer	Boys/Girls 5-14	On-Task Total Problems Internalizing Externalizing Syndromes

SUMMARY

Multiaxial empirically-based assessment emphasizes the use of standardized procedures to identify strengths and weaknesses in terms of five assessment axes: *I. Parent Reports, II. Teacher Reports, III. Cognitive Assessment, IV. Physical Assessment,* and *V. Direct Assessment of the Child.* The five versions of the Child Behavior Checklist are designed to obtain data from parents, teachers, observers, and self-reports. Hand-scored and computer-scored profiles are available for each version.

Our approach to obtaining data from informants for multiaxial empirically-based assessment is characterized by the following features:

1. Syndrome scales for scoring behavioral/emotional problems have been empirically-derived from factor analyses of ratings on large samples of children.

2. Problems and competencies are aggregated into standardized scales.

3. Each instrument is designed for a particular type of informant, and the syndrome scales reflect the patterns found in reports by that type of informant.

4. The diverse items encompassed by the instruments assess a broad range of potential problems.

5. Norms for each instrument show how an informant's reports about a particular child compare with reports by similar informants for large samples of nonreferred children.

6. The instruments are efficient and economical to use, requiring little professional time and enabling practitioners to make better use of face-to-face contacts with clients.

Chapter 3
The Child Behavior Checklist
for Ages 4-16 (CBCL/4-16)

The CBCL/4-16 (blue form) is a four-page form designed to obtain ratings of the competencies and behavioral/emotional problems of children aged 4 through 16, as reported by parents and parent surrogates. The CBCL/4-16 is the original form developed by Achenbach (1978), on which all other versions are based. The CBCL/4-16 can be completed by most parents having at least fifth grade reading skills. Some parents can complete it in as little as 10 minutes, although 15-17 minutes is more typical. Parents provide information for the 20 competence items shown in Figure 3-1, covering their child's activities, involvement with social organizations, social relations, and school performance. They then rate their child on the 118 problem items and 2 open-ended items shown in Figure 3-2, using a 0-1-2 scale for how true the item is of the child now or within the past 6 months. The open-ended items 56h and 113 request parents to describe additional problems not specifically listed. The parent circles a 2 if the item is *very true or often true*; *1* if the item is *somewhat or sometimes true*; or *0* if the item is *not true*.

SCORES AND SCALES OF THE CBCL 4-16

Parents' responses to the CBCL/4-16 are scored on the Child Behavior Profile, which consists of three competence scales and a variety of empirically-derived problem scales, as summarized in Table 3-1. The narrow-band syndrome scales listed in Table 3-1 were derived from factor analyses of CBCLs completed for 2,300 clinically-referred children and normed on 1,300 non-

CHILD BEHAVIOR CHECKLIST FOR AGES 4–16

| For office use only |
| ID # |

CHILD'S NAME

PARENT'S TYPE OF WORK *(Please be specific — for example, auto mechanic, high school teacher, homemaker, laborer, lathe operator, shoe salesman, army sergeant, even if parent does not live with child.)*

SEX ☐ Boy ☐ Girl   AGE   ETHNIC GROUP OR RACE

FATHER'S TYPE OF WORK: _____

MOTHER'S TYPE OF WORK: _____

TODAY'S DATE   CHILD'S BIRTHDATE

THIS FORM FILLED OUT BY:

Mo. _____ Day _____ Yr. _____   Mo. _____ Day _____ Yr. _____

☐ Mother (name): _____

☐ Father (name): _____

GRADE IN SCHOOL

☐ Other — name & relationship to child: _____

I. Please list the sports your child most likes to take part in. For example: swimming, baseball, skating, skate boarding, bike riding, fishing, etc.

☐ None

Compared to other children of the same age, about how much time does he/she spend in each?

Compared to other children of the same age, how well does he/she do each one?

	Don't Know	Less Than Average	Average	More Than Average		Don't Know	Below Average	Average	Above Average
a. _____	☐	☐	☐	☐		☐	☐	☐	☐
b. _____	☐	☐	☐	☐		☐	☐	☐	☐
c. _____	☐	☐	☐	☐		☐	☐	☐	☐

II. Please list your child's favorite hobbies, activities, and games, other than sports. For example: stamps, dolls, books, piano, crafts, singing, etc. (Do not include T.V.)

☐ None

Compared to other children of the same age, about how much time does he/she spend in each?

Compared to other children of the same age, how well does he/she do each one?

	Don't Know	Less Than Average	Average	More Than Average		Don't Know	Below Average	Average	Above Average
a. _____	☐	☐	☐	☐		☐	☐	☐	☐
b. _____	☐	☐	☐	☐		☐	☐	☐	☐
c. _____	☐	☐	☐	☐		☐	☐	☐	☐

III. Please list any organizations, clubs, teams, or groups your child belongs to.

☐ None

Compared to other children of the same age, how active is he/she in each?

	Don't Know	Less Active	Average	More Active
a. _____	☐	☐	☐	☐
b. _____	☐	☐	☐	☐
c. _____	☐	☐	☐	☐

IV. Please list any jobs or chores your child has. For example: paper route, babysitting, making bed, etc.

☐ None

Compared to other children of the same age, how well does he/she carry them out?

	Don't Know	Below Average	Average	Above Average
a. _____	☐	☐	☐	☐
b. _____	☐	☐	☐	☐
c. _____	☐	☐	☐	☐

PAGE 1   3-81 Edition

Figure 3-1. Social competence Items I-IV of the Child Behavior Checklist for Ages 4-16.

V. **1. About how many close friends does your child have?** ☐ None ☐ 1 ☐ 2 or 3 ☐ 4 or more

2. About how many times a week does your child do things with them? ☐ less than 1 ☐ 1 or 2 ☐ 3 or more

VI. Compared to other children of his/her age, how well does your child:

	Worse	About the same	Better
a. Get along with his/her brothers & sisters?	☐	☐	☐
b. Get along with other children?	☐	☐	☐
c. Behave with his/her parents?	☐	☐	☐
d. Play and work by himself/herself?	☐	☐	☐

VII. 1. Current school performance—for children aged 6 and older:

☐ Does not go to school

	Failing	Below average	Average	Above average
a. Reading or English	☐	☐	☐	☐
b. Writing	☐	☐	☐	☐
c. Arithmetic or Math	☐	☐	☐	☐
d. Spelling	☐	☐	☐	☐

Other academic subjects—for example: history, science, foreign language, geography.

	Failing	Below average	Average	Above average
e. _____	☐	☐	☐	☐
f. _____	☐	☐	☐	☐
g. _____	☐	☐	☐	☐

2. Is your child in a special class?

☐ No ☐ Yes—what kind?

3. Has your child ever repeated a grade?

☐ No ☐ Yes—grade and reason

4. Has your child had any academic or other problems in school?

☐ No ☐ Yes—please describe

When did these problems start?

Have these problems ended?

☐ No ☐ Yes—when?

Figure 3-1 (cont.). Social competence Items V-VII of the Child Behavior Checklist for Ages 4-16.

VIII. Below is a list of items that describe children. For each item that describes your child **now or within the past 6 months**, please circle the 2 if the item is **very true** or **often true** of your child. Circle the 1 if the item is **somewhat** or **sometimes true** of your child. If the item is **not true** of your child, circle the 0. Please answer all items as well as you can, even if some do not seem to apply to your child.

0 = Not True (as far as you know)   1 = Somewhat or Sometimes True   2 = Very True or Often True

0 1 2	1.	Acts too young for his/her age	16	0 1 2	31.	Fears he/she might think or do something bad	
0 1 2	2.	Allergy (describe): _____					
				0 1 2	32.	Feels he/she has to be perfect	
		_____		0 1 2	33.	Feels or complains that no one loves him/her	
0 1 2	3.	Argues a lot					
0 1 2	4.	Asthma		0 1 2	34.	Feels others are out to get him/her	
				0 1 2	35.	Feels worthless or inferior	50
0 1 2	5.	Behaves like opposite sex	20				
0 1 2	6.	Bowel movements outside toilet		0 1 2	36.	Gets hurt a lot, accident-prone	
				0 1 2	37.	Gets in many fights	
0 1 2	7.	Bragging, boasting					
0 1 2	8.	Can't concentrate, can't pay attention for long		0 1 2	38.	Gets teased a lot	
				0 1 2	39.	Hangs around with children who get in trouble	
0 1 2	9.	Can't get his/her mind off certain thoughts; obsessions (describe): _____		0 1 2	40.	Hears things that aren't there (describe):	
0 1 2	10.	Can't sit still, restless, or hyperactive	25			_____	55
				0 1 2	41.	Impulsive or acts without thinking	
0 1 2	11.	Clings to adults or too dependent					
0 1 2	12.	Complains of loneliness		0 1 2	42.	Likes to be alone	
				0 1 2	43.	Lying or cheating	
0 1 2	13.	Confused or seems to be in a fog					
0 1 2	14.	Cries a lot		0 1 2	44.	Bites fingernails	
				0 1 2	45.	Nervous, highstrung, or tense	60
0 1 2	15.	Cruel to animals	30				
0 1 2	16.	Cruelty, bullying, or meanness to others		0 1 2	46.	Nervous movements or twitching (describe):	
0 1 2	17.	Day-dreams or gets lost in his/her thoughts				_____	
0 1 2	18.	Deliberately harms self or attempts suicide		0 1 2	47.	Nightmares	
0 1 2	19.	Demands a lot of attention		0 1 2	48.	Not liked by other children	
0 1 2	20.	Destroys his/her own things	35	0 1 2	49.	Constipated, doesn't move bowels	
0 1 2	21.	Destroys things belonging to his/her family or other children		0 1 2	50.	Too fearful or anxious	65
				0 1 2	51.	Feels dizzy	
0 1 2	22.	Disobedient at home					
				0 1 2	52.	Feels too guilty	
0 1 2	23.	Disobedient at school		0 1 2	53.	Overeating	
0 1 2	24.	Doesn't eat well					
				0 1 2	54.	Overtired	
0 1 2	25.	Doesn't get along with other children	40	0 1 2	55.	Overweight	70
0 1 2	26.	Doesn't seem to feel guilty after misbehaving					
					56.	Physical problems without known medical cause:	
0 1 2	27.	Easily jealous		0 1 2	a.	Aches or pains	
0 1 2	28.	Eats or drinks things that are not food (describe): _____		0 1 2	b.	Headaches	
				0 1 2	c.	Nausea, feels sick	
				0 1 2	d.	Problems with eyes (describe): _____	
0 1 2	29.	Fears certain animals, situations, or places, other than school (describe): _____		0 1 2	e.	Rashes or other skin problems	75
				0 1 2	f.	Stomachaches or cramps	
		_____		0 1 2	g.	Vomiting, throwing up	
0 1 2	30.	Fears going to school	45	0 1 2	h.	Other (describe): _____	

Please see other side

PAGE 3

Figure 3-2. Problem items on Page 3 of the Child Behavior Checklist for Ages 4-16.

			0 = Not True (as far as you know)	1 = Somewhat or Sometimes True					2 = Very True or Often True

0	1	2	57.	Physically attacks people		0	1	2	84.	Strange behavior (describe):
0	1	2	58.	Picks nose, skin, or other parts of body (describe):						
				_____ 80		0	1	2	85.	Strange ideas (describe):
0	1	2	59.	Plays with own sex parts in public 16						
0	1	2	60.	Plays with own sex parts too much		0	1	2	86.	Stubborn, sullen, or irritable
0	1	2	61.	Poor school work		0	1	2	87.	Sudden changes in mood or feelings
0	1	2	62.	Poorly coordinated or clumsy		0	1	2	88.	Sulks a lot 45
0	1	2	63.	Prefers playing with older children 20		0	1	2	89.	Suspicious
0	1	2	64.	Prefers playing with younger children		0	1	2	90.	Swearing or obscene language
0	1	2	65.	Refuses to talk		0	1	2	91.	Talks about killing self
0	1	2	66.	Repeats certain acts over and over; compulsions (describe):		0	1	2	92.	Talks or walks in sleep (describe):
						0	1	2	93.	Talks too much 50
0	1	2	67.	Runs away from home		0	1	2	94.	Teases a lot
0	1	2	68.	Screams a lot 25						
						0	1	2	95.	Temper tantrums or hot temper
0	1	2	69.	Secretive, keeps things to self		0	1	2	96.	Thinks about sex too much
0	1	2	70.	Sees things that aren't there (describe):		0	1	2	97.	Threatens people
						0	1	2	98.	Thumb-sucking 55
						0	1	2	99.	Too concerned with neatness or cleanliness
						0	1	2	100.	Trouble sleeping (describe):
0	1	2	71.	Self-conscious or easily embarrassed						
0	1	2	72.	Sets fires						
0	1	2	73.	Sexual problems (describe):		0	1	2	101.	Truancy, skips school
						0	1	2	102.	Underactive, slow moving, or lacks energy
				_____ 30		0	1	2	103.	Unhappy, sad, or depressed 60
0	1	2	74.	Showing off or clowning		0	1	2	104.	Unusually loud
0	1	2	75.	Shy or timid		0	1	2	105.	Uses alcohol or drugs (describe):
0	1	2	76.	Sleeps less than most children						
0	1	2	77.	Sleeps more than most children during day and/or night (describe):		0	1	2	106.	Vandalism
						0	1	2	107.	Wets self during the day
						0	1	2	108.	Wets the bed 65
0	1	2	78.	Smears or plays with bowel movements 35		0	1	2	109.	Whining
						0	1	2	110.	Wishes to be of opposite sex
0	1	2	79.	Speech problem (describe):		0	1	2	111.	Withdrawn, doesn't get involved with others
						0	1	2	112.	Worrying
0	1	2	80.	Stares blankly					113.	Please write in any problems your child has that were not listed above:
0	1	2	81.	Steals at home						
0	1	2	82.	Steals outside the home		0	1	2		_____ 70
0	1	2	83.	Stores up things he/she doesn't need (describe):		0	1	2		
				_____ 40		0	1	2		

PLEASE BE SURE YOU HAVE ANSWERED ALL ITEMS.   PAGE 4   UNDERLINE ANY YOU ARE CONCERNED ABOUT.

Figure 3-2 (cont.). Problem items on Page 4 of the Child Behavior Checklist for Ages 4-16.

Table 3-1
Scales Scored from the Child Behavior Checklist for Ages 4-16[a]

Total Competence	Total Problems
Activities	Internalizing
Social	Externalizing
School	

Narrow-Band Syndromes

Boys 4-5	*Girls 4-5*
Social Withdrawal	Somatic Complaints
Depressed	Depressed
Immature	Schizoid or Anxious
Somatic Complaints	Social Withdrawal
Sex Problems	Obese
Schizoid	Aggressive
Aggressive	Sex Problems
Delinquent	Hyperactive

Boys 6-11	*Girls 6-11*
Schizoid or Anxious	Depressed
Depressed	Social Withdrawal
Uncommunicative	Somatic Complaints
Obsessive-Compulsive	Schizoid-Obsessive
Somatic Complaints	Hyperactive
Social Withdrawal	Sex Problems
Hyperactive	Delinquent
Aggressive	Aggressive
Delinquent	Cruel

Boys 12-16	*Girls 12-16*
Somatic Complaints	Anxious-Obsessive
Schizoid	Somatic Complaints
Uncommunicative	Schizoid
Immature	Depressed Withdrawal
Obsessive-Compulsive	Immature Hyperactive
Hostile Withdrawal	Delinquent
Delinquent	Aggressive
Aggressive	Cruel
Hyperactive	

[a]Scales were derived from parents' ratings of 2,300 clinically-referred children and normed on 1,300 nonreferred children.

referred children. The scoring profiles for the CBCL/4-16 are standardized separately for each sex in the age ranges shown in Table 3-1. The reader should refer to the *Manual for the Child Behavior Checklist* (Achenbach & Edelbrock, 1983) for details of scoring procedures, as well as data on reliability, validity, standardization samples, and other information on development and applications.

Beside scores on the various competence and problem scales, the computer-scored version of the CBCL/4-16 profile compares a child's overall pattern of problems with profile types identified through hierarchical cluster analyses (Achenbach & Edelbrock, 1983; Edelbrock & Achenbach, 1980). Either six or seven profile types were found for each sex/age group. An intraclass correlation coefficient (ICC) printed on the computer-scored profile indicates the degree of similarity between the child's profile and each of the profile types identified for his/her sex and age. The *Manual for the Child Behavior Checklist* presents details of the profile types.

Competence Scales

Figure 3-3 shows the hand-scored version of the competence scales of the CBCL/4-16 for Michael, an 11-year-old boy, while Table 3-2 explains each score in the profile. The procedures for hand scoring each of the competence scales are described in the *Manual* for the CBCL.

On the profile shown in Figure 3-3, Michael's total competence score of 9.5 was in the clinical range compared to norms for nonreferred boys aged 6-11 ($T = 25$; <10th percentile). His score of 6.5 on the Activities scale was in the normal range (T score = 44; >2nd percentile). His score of 2.0 on the Social scale, however, was in the clinical range (T score = 21; <2nd percentile), as was his score of 1.0 on the School scale (T score = 20; <2nd percentile). On the Social scale, Michael's mother reported that he belonged to no social organizations or groups and had only one friend. She rated him worse than other children in getting along with other children, behaving with parents, and

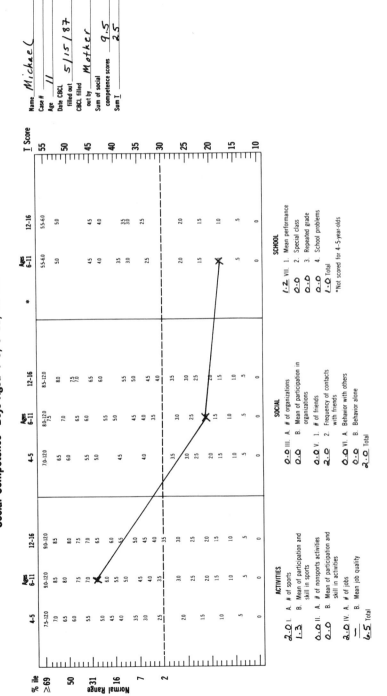

Figure 3-3. Hand-scored version of the CBCL/4-16 competence scales for 11-year-old Michael. Note that the clinical cutoff is the 10th percentile for the total competence score and the 2nd percentile for the competence scales.

Table 3-2
Explanations of Scores on the Competence Scales
of the Child Behavior Profile

Percentiles: the percent of children in the normative sample of nonreferred children who obtained a score less than or equal to each raw score.

T **scores:** standard scores based on the percentiles of the raw scores for normative samples of nonreferred children. The normalized *T* scores have means near 50 and standard deviations near 7, but these vary among the scales, because of skewed distributions of raw scores.

Normal range: scores at and above the broken line that marks the 2nd percentile of the normative sample. Scores below the broken line are considered to be in the clinical range on the competence scales. The scores are truncated at the 69th percentile (*T* = 55) to prevent overinterpretation of differences among scores at the high end of the normal range.

Activities total: raw score obtained by summing the six scores entered on the Activities scale, rounded to the nearest .5.

Activities *T* score: normalized *T* score for Activities scale based on the normative sample of nonreferred children.

Social total: raw score obtained by summing the six scores entered on the Social scale, rounded to the nearest .5.

Social *T* score: normalized *T* score for Social scale based on the normative sample of nonreferred children.

School total: raw score obtained by summing the four scores entered on the School scale, rounded to the nearest .5.

School *T* score: normalized *T* score for School scale based on the normative sample of nonreferred children.

Sum of social competence scores: total competence raw score obtained by summing the totals of the Activities, Social, and School scales. Scores below the 10th percentile are considered to be in the clinical range.

Sum *T*: normalized *T* score for total competence based on the normative sample of nonreferred children.

playing and working by himself. On the School scale, Michael's mother rated his school performance below average in all subjects except science. She also reported that he was in a special class for reading, had repeated first and third grade, and had problems getting along with others in school.

Figure 3-4 shows the computer-scored version for the same profile of competence scales for 11-year-old Michael.

Problem Scales

Figure 3-5 shows the hand-scored version of the problem scales of the CBCL/4-16 for 11-year-old Michael, while Table 3-3 explains each score in the profile. The procedures for hand-scoring the problem scales are described in the *Manual* for the CBCL/4-16.

On the profile in Figure 3-5, Michael's total problem score of 95 (designated as *Sum* in upper righthand corner) was in the clinical range compared to norms for boys 6-11 ($T = 81$; >90th percentile), as were his scores on both the Internalizing ($T = 72$; >90th percentile) and Externalizing scales ($T = 82$; >90th percentile). Scores on the Depressed, Uncommunicative, Obsessive-Compulsive, Social Withdrawal, Hyperactive, Aggressive, and Delinquent scales were all in the clinical range (T scores = 71 to 86; >98th percentile). The Depressed scale included scores for items such as *14. Cries a lot*; *18. Deliberately harms self or attempts suicide*; *88. Sulks a lot*; and *103. Unhappy, sad or depressed.* The Uncommunicative scale included *13. Confused or seems to be in a fog*; *69. Secretive, keeps things to self* and *86. Stubborn, sullen or irritable.* The Obsessive-Compulsive scale included *9. Can't get his mind off certain thoughts, obsessions*; *66. Repeats certain acts over and over, compulsions*; *83. Stores up things he doesn't need*; and *85. Strange ideas.* The Social Withdrawal scale included *25. Doesn't get along with other children*; *34. Feels others are out to get him*; and *48. Not liked by other children.* The Hyperactive scale included *1. Acts too young for his age*; *8. Can't concentrate, can't pay attention for long*; and *10. Can't sit still, restless, or hyperactive.* The

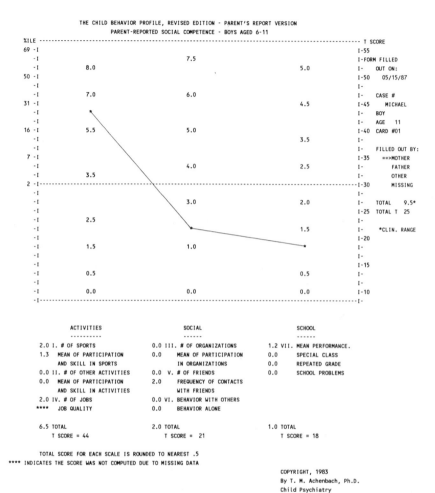

THE CHILD BEHAVIOR PROFILE, REVISED EDITION - PARENT'S REPORT VERSION
PARENT-REPORTED SOCIAL COMPETENCE - BOYS AGED 6-11

	ACTIVITIES		SOCIAL		SCHOOL
	----------		------		------
2.0	I. # OF SPORTS	0.0	III. # OF ORGANIZATIONS	1.2	VII. MEAN PERFORMANCE.
1.3	MEAN OF PARTICIPATION	0.0	MEAN OF PARTICIPATION	0.0	SPECIAL CLASS
	AND SKILL IN SPORTS		IN ORGANIZATIONS	0.0	REPEATED GRADE
0.0	II. # OF OTHER ACTIVITIES	0.0	V. # OF FRIENDS	0.0	SCHOOL PROBLEMS
0.0	MEAN OF PARTICIPATION	2.0	FREQUENCY OF CONTACTS		
	AND SKILL IN ACTIVITIES		WITH FRIENDS		
2.0	IV. # OF JOBS	0.0	VI. BEHAVIOR WITH OTHERS		
****	JOB QUALITY	0.0	BEHAVIOR ALONE		
6.5	TOTAL	2.0	TOTAL	1.0	TOTAL
	T SCORE = 44		T SCORE = 21		T SCORE = 18

TOTAL SCORE FOR EACH SCALE IS ROUNDED TO NEAREST .5
**** INDICATES THE SCORE WAS NOT COMPUTED DUE TO MISSING DATA

Figure 3-4. Computer-scored version of the CBCL/4-16 competence scales for 11-year-old Michael.

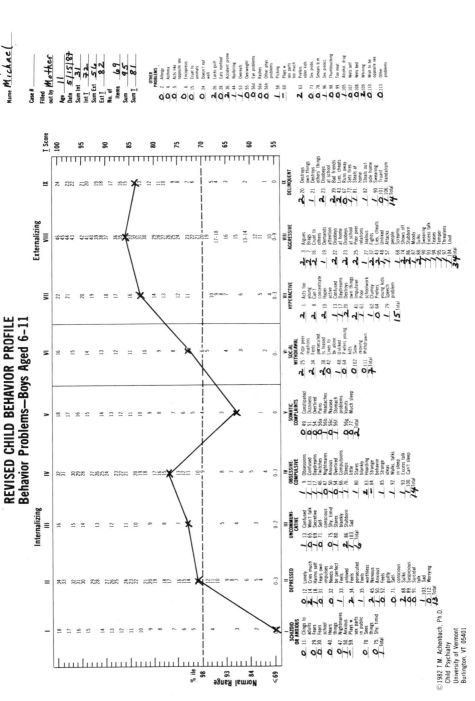

Figure 3-5. Hand-scored version of the CBCL/4-16 problem scales for 11-year-old Michael. Note that the clinical cutoff is the 90th percentile for the total problem score and the 98th percentile for the narrow-band scales.

Table 3-3
Explanations of Scores on the Problem Scales
of the Child Behavior Profile

Percentiles: the percent of children in the normative sample of nonreferred children who obtained a score less than or equal to each raw score.

T **scores:** normalized standard scores based on the percentiles of raw scores for nonreferred children. The normalized *T* scores have means near 57 and standard deviations near 5, but these vary slightly among scales, because of skewed distributions of raw scores.

Normal range: scores at and below the broken line that marks the 98th percentile of the normative sample. Scores above the broken line are considered to be in the clinical range. The range of scores is truncated at a score of 55 to prevent over-interpretation of differences among scores at the low end of the normal range.

Narrow-band scale total: raw score obtained by summing the 0s, 1s, and 2s entered for each item on the scale.

Narrow-band *T* score: normalized *T* score based on the percentiles of raw scores for nonreferred children.

Sum Int: Internalizing raw score obtained by summing the 0s, 1s, and 2s of the Internalizing items listed in the first column on the right side of the profile (not shown in Fig. 3-5). Scores above the 90th percentile are considered to be in the clinical range.

Int *T*: normalized *T* score for the Internalizing scale based on the raw scores for the normative sample of nonreferred children.

Sum Ext: Externalizing raw score obtained by summing the 0s, 1s, and 2s of the Externalizing items listed in the second column on the right side of the profile (not shown in Fig. 3-5). Scores above the 90th percentile are considered to be in the clinical range.

Ext *T*: normalized *T* score for the Externalizing scale based on the raw scores for the normative sample of nonreferred children.

Sum: total problem raw score obtained by summing the 0s, 1s, and 2s for all of the specific problem items. Scores above the 90th percentile are considered to be in the clinical range.

Sum *T*: normalized *T* score for the total problem score based on the raw scores for the normative sample of nonreferred children.

Other problems: scores of 0, 1, or 2 for items counted in the total problem score, but not included in scores for any of the narrow-band scales.

Aggressive and Delinquent scales included many items covering verbal and physical aggression and violations of social rules, such as *3. Argues a lot*; *22. Disobedient at home*; *37. Gets in many fights*; *43. Lying or cheating*; *94. Teases a lot*; *95. Temper tantrums or hot temper*; *81. Steals at home*; *82. Steals outside the home*; and *106. Vandalism.*

Figure 3-6 shows the computer-scored version of the same problem profile for 11-year-old Michael. In addition to all of the scores listed above, the computer-scored version provides clinical *T* scores for narrow-band scales to allow comparisons of the child to clinically-referred children as well as to the normative sample. As explained earlier, the computer-scored version also lists intraclass correlations with profile types. Table 3-4 explains the clinical *T* scores and intraclass correlations. The intraclass correlations shown in Figure 3-6 indicate that Michael's profile was most like that of clinically-referred boys with the Hyperactive (ICC = .380) and Delinquent (ICC = .497) profile types.

Table 3-4
Explanations of Additional Scores on the Problem Scales of the Computer-Scored Child Behavior Profile

---

Narrow-band clinic T score: *T* score based on raw scores obtained by a sample of clinically-referred children of the same sex and age range. Clinic *T* scores are obtained only through computer scoring.

Intraclass corr: the intraclass correlation showing the similarity of an individual child's profile of problems to profile types identified by cluster analyses for each sex/age group. Because the intraclass correlation is computed from conversion of the child's raw scale scores to clinic *T* scores, the pattern of these *T* scores may differ from the pattern of the norm-based *T* scores visible in the graphic display of the child's profile. The intraclass correlations with profile types can be obtained only through computer-scoring.

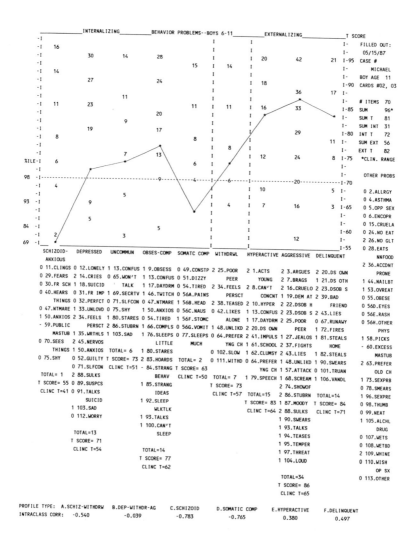

Figure 3-6. Computer-scored version of the CBCL/4-16 problem scales for 11-year-old Michael.

Summary of Cutoff Scores

To provide a quick reference for the practitioner, Table 3-5 summarizes the cutoffs between the normal and clinical range for the scales of the CBCL/4-16. Cutoffs are listed in terms of raw scores and percentiles for total competence and total problem scores for each sex/age group. Cutoffs for the remaining competence scales, Internalizing, Externalizing, and nar-

Table 3-5
Clinical Cutoff Points for CBCL/4-16 Scales

Scale	Group	Raw Score	T Score	Percentile
Total Competence[a]	Boys 4-5	9.5	c	10
	Boys 6-11	16.0	c	10
	Boys 12-16	16.0	c	10
	Girls 4-5	10.0	c	10
	Girls 6-11	16.5	c	10
	Girls 12-16	16.5	c	10
Activities, Social, School[a]	All groups	Varies	30	2
Total Problems[b]	Boys 4-5	42	c	90
	Boys 6-11	40	c	90
	Boys 12-16	38	c	90
	Girls 4-5	42	c	88
	Girls 6-11	37	c	90
	Girls 12-16	37	c	90
Internalizing, Externalizing[b]	All groups	Varies	63	90
Narrow-band Syndromes[b]	All groups	Varies	70	98

[a]Scores *below* the cutoffs are in the clinical range.
[b]Scores *above* the cutoffs are in the clinical range.
[c]The raw score, not the T score, is used as the clinical cutoff on this scale, since more than one raw score corresponds to the same T score for some groups.

row-band problem scales are given only in terms of T scores and percentiles for all groups, since raw score cutoffs vary across these scales.

The clinical cutoffs are set at the 10th percentile for total competence and the 90th percentile for total problems, Internalizing, and Externalizing, because these points were efficient discriminators between clinically-referred and nonreferred children. The one exception is the total problem score for girls aged 4-5, where the 88th percentile was a more efficient discriminator. Cutoffs on the three competence scales and the narrow-band problem scales are set at more extreme levels (2nd and 98th percentiles respectively) because the smaller number of items comprising each of these scales argued for a more conservative standard for judging deviance than on the total problems, Internalizing, and Externalizing scales.

MULTIAXIAL EMPIRICALLY-BASED ASSESS-MENT INITIATED WITH THE CBCL

To provide an overview of multiaxial empirically-based assessment initiated with the CBCL, Figure 3-7 illustrates a typical sequence beginning with the parent as the first major informant. The sequence includes referral, data gathering, data integration, case management, and outcome evaluation. Parents are usually the first contacts in cases referred to outpatient clinics, hospitals, and private practitioners, as well as in some referrals to school personnel. In these contexts, the CBCL can serve as a routine part of the initial data gathering. Prior to the intake interview, the CBCL can be mailed to parents, along with a history form for obtaining information on the child's development, and relevant permission and release forms. If it is not practical to mail the forms in advance, they can be filled out in a waiting room. If both parents are available, it is helpful to have each one complete a separate CBCL and to compare the resulting profiles.

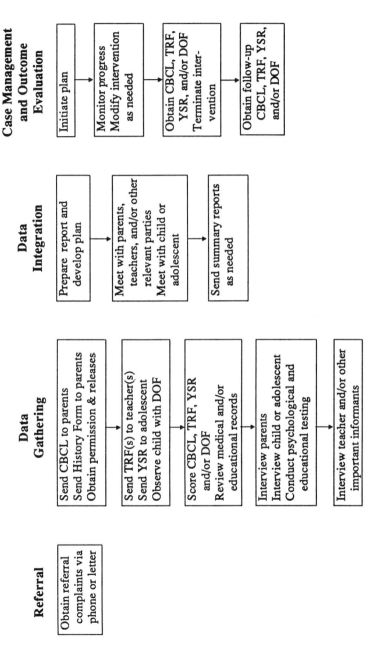

Figure 3-7. Illustrative sequence of empirically-based assessment where the parent is the first informant.

With permission from the parents, the TRF can be sent to the child's teacher. If the child has more than one teacher, it is helpful to obtain TRFs from those having the most contact with the child in different types of classes. The YSR can also be completed by adolescents aged 11 to 18. Mailing the YSR separately to older adolescents with a separate return envelope beside the one provided for parents can help to protect the privacy of the self-report. If the referral complaints include school problems, it might also be appropriate to arrange for observations of the child in the classroom using the DOF. The use of the TRF, YSR, and DOF would depend on the reason for referral. For example, parents bringing their child to a mental health practitioner for help in dealing with a divorce or child abuse might not want the school contacted.

The CBCL, TRF, YSR, and DOF can provide a wealth of information about the child's functioning from multiple perspectives. This information enables the practitioner to determine whether the problems reported deviate from norms for nonreferred agemates of the same sex. If there are major disagreements between profiles, these can be explored in the interview with the parents and/or other referral sources. The practitioner should also review relevant medical and educational records to learn the child's history and determine if any additional information is needed.

Based on the intake information, the practitioner can tailor interviews with parents and other informants to address the main areas of concern and explore issues that would be most helpful in designing interventions. Children and adolescents are often interviewed after their parents, but in some cases, it may be preferable to interview adolescents before the parents or jointly with the parents. With the CBCL and other measures scored in advance, the practitioner can address the identified problems in the interview with the child or adolescent and obtain his/her perspective on them. If the YSR has been completed, it provides a good take-off point for interviewing adolescents, especially because adolescents often spontaneously elaborate on their YSR responses. If they do not, they can be asked to tell more about problems they have scored as present or descriptions that they have added to items. Items concerning harm to self or others and items concerning markedly deviant thoughts, feelings, and behavior are especially important candidates for discussion. Psychological and educational testing can either follow or precede the interview, depending on the practitioner's judgment. Contacts with teachers can focus on TRF results and other school-related concerns.

After all the assessment data have been gathered, they must be integrated to form a plan of action, which is usually embodied in an evaluation report. Chapter 8 presents examples of reports integrating results from the CBCL, TRF, YSR, and DOF with other findings. Although each instrument is tailored to a different type of informant, the overlaps in items and types of scores enable the practitioner to compare the pictures provided by the various informants. This can be done in terms of total scores, profiles, and individual items. Recommendations can then take account of different perspectives on the child's functioning and variations in problems and competencies across different environments and interaction partners. Such comparisons of results on the empirically-based measures, in turn, facilitate selecting targets for change. Recommendations are usually discussed with parents, the child or adolescent, and other closely involved people, such as teachers or case workers. This is best accomplished in face-to-face meetings to encourage responses to recommendations and discussion of further concerns and plans.

Once a plan has been initiated, the practitioner should monitor the child's progress and modify interventions as needed. To do this, one or more of the empirically-based measures can be repeated after interventions have had time to take effect. It may also be appropriate to monitor progress with other forms of assessment, such as achievement tests or scales targeted at specific problems, such as hyperactivity or depression. After 3 months or more, the practitioner can obtain the CBCL again from the parents to compare it with the original CBCL. It may also be appropriate to obtain the TRF from teachers, the YSR from adolescents, and the DOF from an observer. Comparisons of profiles before and after an intervention will enable the practitioner to determine whether the approaches taken have been effective and when it is appropriate to terminate the intervention. If improvements have not occurred, interventions may need to be modified and the effects of revised approaches monitored. After an intervention has been terminated, follow-up evaluations are desirable at regular intervals, such as 6, 12, or 18 months. This can be done by having any available informants complete the appropriate forms. Follow-up evaluations are important not only to ensure that referred children have really improved, but also to help practitioners determine which interventions are most effective with which types of cases.

SUMMARY

The CBCL/4-16 is designed to obtain parents' ratings of the competencies and problems of 4- to 16-year-olds. It is the form on which all the other versions of the CBCL are based. Parents' responses to the CBCL are scored on the Child Behavior Profile, which consists of competence scales and empirically-derived problem scales standardized separately for each sex at ages 4-5, 6-11, and 12-16. Beside providing scores for all scales, the computer-scored version of the profile provides intraclass correlations between a child's pattern of problems and the profile types that we have identified through cluster analyses.

All scales scored from the CBCL/4-16 are listed in Table 3-1, while cutoff scores for distinguishing between the normal and clinical ranges are listed in Table 3-5. Figure 3-7 illustrates a sequence of multiaxial empirically-based assessment initiated with the CBCL, including referral, data gathering, data integration, case management, and outcome evaluation.

Chapter 4
The Child Behavior Checklist for
Ages 2-3 (CBCL/2-3)

The CBCL/2-3 (blue form) is a two-page form designed to obtain parents' ratings of children aged 2-3 years. Modeled on the problem portion of the CBCL/4-16 for rating older children, it consists of 99 items describing behavioral/emotional problems, plus an open-ended item for additional problems. Fifty-nine of the items have counterparts on the CBCL/4-16, while the remaining items are designed specifically for the younger age group. Parents rate their child on each item that describes the child currently or within the last 2 months. The 2-month rating period was chosen in preference to the 6-month period of the CBCL/4-16 to take account of the faster pace of change likely to be found during the early years. The parent circles a 2 if the item is *very true or often true*; *1* if the item is *somewhat or sometimes true*; or *0* if the item is *not true*. Figure 4-1 shows the CBCL/2-3, indicating the items that differ from the CBCL/4-16. (The CBCL/2-3 does not have competence items.)

SCORES AND SCALES OF THE CBCL/2-3

Parents' responses to the CBCL/2-3 are scored on the Child Behavior Profile for Ages 2-3. This profile includes six narrow-band syndrome scales derived from factor analyses of 398 CBCLs for nonreferred children as well as children referred for mental health services or considered at risk for problems because of low birthweight. Scales were normed on 273 randomly--selected nonreferred children. Because no sex differences were found in scale scores, 2-3-year-olds of both sexes are scored on

CHILD BEHAVIOR CHECKLIST FOR AGES 2-3

For office use only
ID #

CHILD'S NAME

PARENT'S TYPE OF WORK *(Please be specific—for example, auto mechanic, high school teacher, homemaker, laborer, lathe operator, shoe salesman, army sergeant, even if parent does not live with child.)*

SEX ☐ Boy   ☐ Girl   AGE   ETHNIC GROUP OR RACE

FATHER'S TYPE OF WORK:_____

MOTHER'S TYPE OF WORK:_____

TODAY'S DATE   CHILD'S BIRTHDATE

Mo._____ Day_____ Yr._____   Mo._____ Day_____ Yr._____

THIS FORM FILLED OUT BY:

☐ Mother (name):_____

☐ Father (name):_____

☐ Other — name & relationship to child:

Please fill out this form to reflect *your* view of the child's behavior even if other people might not agree about the behavior.

Below is a list of items that describe children. For each item that describes the child **now or within the past 2 months**, please circle the **2** if the item is **very true** or **often true** of the child. Circle the **1** if the item is **somewhat** or **sometimes true** of the child. If the item is **not true** of the child, circle the **0**. Please answer all items as well as you can, even if some do not seem to apply to the child.

0 = Not True (as far as you know)   1 = Somewhat or Sometimes True   2 = Very True or Often True

0 1 2 1. Aches or pains (without medical cause)	0 1 2 ᵃ 33. Feelings are easily hurt
0 1 2 2. Acts too young for age	0 1 2 34. Gets hurt a lot, accident-prone
0 1 2 ᵃ 3. Afraid to try new things	0 1 2 35. Gets in many fights
0 1 2 ᵃ 4. Avoids looking others in the eye	0 1 2 ᵃ 36. Gets into everything
0 1 2 5. Can't concentrate, can't pay attention for long	0 1 2 ᵃ 37. Gets too upset when separated from parents
0 1 2 ᵇ 6. Can't sit still or restless	0 1 2 ᵇ 38. Has trouble getting to sleep
0 1 2 ᵃ 7. Can't stand having things out of place	0 1 2 39. Headaches (without medical cause)
0 1 2 ᵃ 8. Can't stand waiting; wants everything now	0 1 2 ᵃ 40. Hits others
0 1 2 ᵃ 9. Chews on things that aren't edible	0 1 2 ᵃ 41. Holds his/her breath
0 1 2 10. Clings to adults or too dependent	0 1 2 ᵃ 42. Hurts animals or people without meaning to
0 1 2 ᵃ 11. Constantly seeks help	0 1 2 ᵃ 43. Looks unhappy without good reason
0 1 2 12. Constipated, doesn't move bowels	0 1 2 ᵃ 44. Angry moods
0 1 2 13. Cries a lot	0 1 2 45. Nausea, feels sick (without medical cause)
0 1 2 14. Cruel to animals	0 1 2 46. Nervous movements or twitching
0 1 2 ᵃ 15. Defiant	(describe): _____
0 1 2 ᵃ 16. Demands must be met immediately	
0 1 2 17. Destroys his/her own things	0 1 2 47. Nervous, highstrung, or tense
0 1 2 18. Destroys things belonging to his/her family or	0 1 2 48. Nightmares
other children	0 1 2 49. Overeating
0 1 2 ᵃ 19. Diarrhea or loose bowels when not sick	0 1 2 50. Overtired
0 1 2 ᵇ 20. Disobedient	0 1 2 51. Overweight
0 1 2 ᵃ 21. Disturbed by any change in routine	0 1 2 ᵃ 52. Painful bowel movements
0 1 2 ᵃ 22. Doesn't want to sleep alone	0 1 2 53. Physically attacks people
0 1 2 ᵃ 23. Doesn't answer when people talk to him/her	0 1 2 54. Picks nose, skin, or other parts of body
0 1 2 ᵇ 24. Doesn't eat well (describe): _____	(describe): _____
0 1 2 25. Doesn't get along with other children	0 1 2 55. Plays with own sex parts too much
0 1 2 ᵃ 26. Doesn't know how to have fun, acts like a little	0 1 2 56. Poorly coordinated or clumsy
adult	0 1 2 57. Problems with eyes without medical cause
0 1 2 27. Doesn't seem to feel guilty after misbehaving	(describe): _____
0 1 2 ᵃ 28. Doesn't want to go out of home	
0 1 2 ᵃ 29. Easily frustrated	0 1 2 ᵃ 58. Punishment doesn't change his/her behavior
0 1 2 30. Easily jealous	0 1 2 ᵃ 59. Quickly shifts from one activity to another
0 1 2 31. Eats or drinks things that are not food	0 1 2 60. Rashes or other skin problems (without
(describe): _____	medical cause)
	0 1 2 ᵃ 61. Refuses to eat
0 1 2 ᵇ 32. Fears certain animals, situations, or places	0 1 2 ᵃ 62. Refuses to play active games
(describe): _____	0 1 2 ᵃ 63. Repeatedly rocks head or body
	0 1 2 ᵃ 64. Resists going to bed at night

PAGE 1   **Please see other side**

Figure 4-1. Page 1 of the Child Behavior Checklist for Ages 2-3. Items marked *a* replace CBCL/4-16 items, while items marked *b* differ slightly from CBCL/4-16 items. Note that item numbers on the CBCL/2-3 differ from those on the CBCL/4-16.

0 = Not True (as far as you know)   1 = Somewhat or Sometimes True   2 = Very True or Often True

0	1	2	a 65. Resists toilet training (describe): _____		0	1	2	82. Sudden changes in mood or feelings
			_____		0	1	2	83. Sulks a lot
0	1	2	66. Screams a lot		0	1	2 b	84. Talks or cries out in sleep
0	1	2	a 67. Seems unresponsive to affection		0	1	2	85. Temper tantrums or hot temper
0	1	2	68. Self-conscious or easily embarrassed		0	1	2	86. Too concerned with neatness or cleanliness
0	1	2	a 69. Selfish or won't share		0	1	2	87. Too fearful or anxious
0	1	2	a 70. Shows little affection toward people		0	1	2 a	88. Uncooperative
0	1	2	a 71. Shows little interest in things around him/her		0	1	2	89. Underactive, slow moving, or lacks energy
0	1	2	a 72. Shows too little fear of getting hurt		0	1	2	90. Unhappy, sad, or depressed
0	1	2	73. Shy or timid		0	1	2	91. Unusually loud
0	1	2	74. Sleeps less than most children during day		0	1	2 a	92. Upset by new people or situations
			and/or night (describe): _____					(describe): _____
			_____					_____
0	1	2	75. Smears or plays with bowel movements		0	1	2	93. Vomiting, throwing up (without medical cause)
0	1	2	76. Speech problem (describe): _____		0	1	2 a	94. Wakes up often at night
			_____		0	1	2 a	95. Wanders away from home
0	1	2	b 77. Stares into space or seems preoccupied		0	1	2	96. Wants a lot of attention
0	1	2	78. Stomachaches or cramps (without medical		0	1	2 b	96. Wants a lot of attention
			cause)		0	1	2	97. Whining
0	1	2	79. Stores up things he/she doesn't need		0	1	2	98. Withdrawn, doesn't get involved with others
			(describe): _____		0	1	2	99. Worrying
			_____				100.	Please write in any problems your child has
0	1	2	80. Strange behavior (describe): _____					that were not listed above.
			_____		0	1	2	_____
0	1	2	81. Stubborn, sullen, or irritable		0	1	2	_____
					0	1	2	_____

PLEASE BE SURE YOU HAVE ANSWERED ALL ITEMS.   UNDERLINE ANY YOU ARE CONCERNED ABOUT.

Figure 4-1 (cont.). Page 2 of the Child Behavior Checklist for Ages 2-3. Items marked *a* replace CBCL/4-16 items, while items marked *b* differ slightly from CBCL/4-16 items. Note that item numbers on the CBCL/2-3 differ from those on the CBCL/4-16.

the same profile. Table 4-1 summarizes the scales of the CBCL/2-3, while Table 4-2 lists the mean scores and standard deviations obtained by normative and clinical samples on each scale. Achenbach, Edelbrock, and Howell (1987) provide details of reliability, validity, characteristics of the standardization samples, and other information on the development of the CBCL/2-3.

Table 4-1
Scales Scored from the Child Behavior Checklist for Ages 2-3[a]

Total Problems
Internalizing
Externalizing

Narrow-Band Syndromes

Social Withdrawal
Depressed
Sleep Problems
Somatic Problems
Aggressive
Destructive

[a]Scales derived from factor analysis of parents' ratings of 398 nonreferred, clinically-referred, and at-risk children and normed on 273 nonreferred children.

Problem Scales

Figure 4-2 shows the hand-scored version of the CBCL/2-3 profile for Bobby, a 3-year-old boy. The layout of the computer- scored version is similar to that shown in Figure 3-6 for the CBCL/4-16. The types of scores and cutoffs are analogous to those described in Chapter 3 for the problem portion of the CBCL/4-16.

Table 4-2
Means and Standard Deviations for CBCL/2-3 Scales

	Normative Sample $N = 273$				Clinical Sample $N = 96$			
	Raw Scores		T Scores		Raw Scores		T Scores	
Scales	Mean	S.D.	Mean	S.D.	Mean	S.D.	Mean	S.D.
Total Problems	40.6	19.5	50.3	9.8	70.5	27.2	63.8	11.4
Internalizing	7.9	5.8	51.2	9.7	13.7	9.1	59.5	12.9
Externalizing	22.5	11.8	50.6	9.9	33.2	16.2	58.8	12.4
Social Withdrawal	5.5	3.8	57.4	4.5	7.7	5.4	60.3	8.5
Depressed	2.9	3.2	57.3	4.3	6.9	6.0	62.9	9.1
Sleep Problems	4.2	3.1	57.7	5.5	6.6	4.6	62.7	10.5
Somatic Problems	2.7	2.2	57.6	4.8	4.3	4.7	60.6	8.3
Aggressive	20.6	10.6	57.2	4.7	30.4	14.4	62.8	9.6
Destructive	4.7	3.5	57.4	4.5	6.9	5.0	60.8	7.9

Note. Sample characteristics described by Achenbach, Edelbrock, and Howell (1987).

On the profile shown in Figure 4-2, Bobby obtained a total problem score of 75 (designated as *Sum* in upper righthand corner), which was in the clinical range compared to norms for parents' ratings of nonreferred 2-3-year-olds (*T* score = 65; >90th percentile). His Externalizing score of 52 was also in the clinical range (*T* score = 72; >90th percentile), but his Internalizing score of 9 was well within the normal range (*T* score = 55; <90th percentile). Bobby's score of 46 on the Aggressive scale fell just at the clinical cutoff (*T* score = 70; 98th percentile), with scores of 1 or 2 on items such as *6. Can't sit still or restless*; *15. Defiant*; *20. Disobedient*; *35. Gets in many fights*; *36. Gets into everything*; and *85. Temper tantrums or hot temper*. Scores on all other scales were in the normal range (<98th percentile), though his *T* score on the Destructive scale was relatively high compared to his scores on the remaining scales.

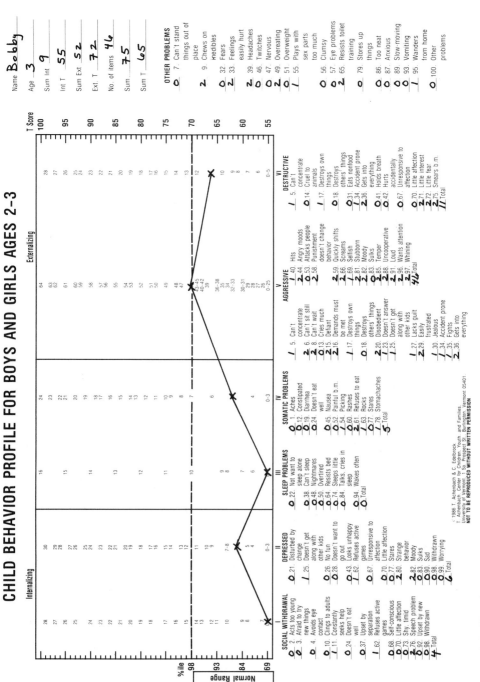

Figure 4-2. Hand-scored version of CBCL/2-3 profile for 3-year-old Bobby. Note that the clinical cutoff is the 90th percentile for the total problem score and the 98th percentile for the narrow-band scales.

Summary of Cutoffs

Table 4-3 lists the clinical cutoffs for the total problem score in terms of raw scores and percentiles. Cutoffs for the narrow-band scales are listed only in terms of T scores and percentiles, since raw score cutoffs vary across these scales. As with the CBCL/4-16, the clinical cutoffs for the narrow-band scales are set at a higher level (98th percentile) than for the total problem score, Internalizing, and Externalizing (90th percentile) because there are fewer items on each of the narrow-band scales.

Table 4-3
Clinical Cutoff Points for CBCL/2-3 Scales

Scale	Raw Score	T score	Percentile
Total Problems[a]	63	b	90
Internalizing[a]	16	63	90
Externalizing[a]	37	b	90
Narrow-band Syndromes[a]	Varies	70	98

[a]Scores *above* the cutoffs are in the clinical range.
[b]The raw score, not the T score, is used as the clinical cutoff on this scale, since more than one raw score corresponds to the same T score.

SUMMARY

The CBCL/2-3 is designed to obtain parents' ratings of the behavioral/emotional problems of 2-3-year-olds. It is scored on the Child Behavior Profile for Ages 2-3, which consists of syndrome scales derived empirically for both sexes combined and scored the same way for both sexes, since no sex differences were found in the distribution of scores. Table 4-2 lists mean scores for the normative sample and a clinical sample on each scale, while Table 4-3 lists cutoff points for distinguishing between the normal and clinical ranges.

Chapter 5
The Teacher's Report Form (TRF)

The TRF (green form) is a four-page form designed to obtain teachers' reports of children's school performance, adaptive functioning, and behavioral/emotional problems. Figure 5-1 shows the adaptive functioning portion of the TRF. School performance is rated on a 5-point scale ranging from 1 (far below grade level) to 5 (far above grade level) for each academic subject. For adaptive functioning, teachers rate children on 7-point scales in four areas: how hard the child is working; how appropriately he/she is behaving; how much he/she is learning; and how happy he/she is. Teachers then rate the child on 118 specific problem items, plus two open-ended items, using a 0-1-2 scale for how true the item is of the child now or within the past 2 months. The 2-month period was chosen in preference to longer rating periods, because longer periods would reduce the portion of the school year during which ratings could be made and because teachers are not apt to remember the specific behaviors of individual children over longer periods. The teacher circles a 2 if the item is *very true or often true*; *1* if the item is *somewhat or sometimes true*; or *0* if the item is *not true*. Ninety-three items have counterparts on the CBCL/4-16 rated by parents, while the remaining items concern school behaviors that parents would not observe, such as difficulty following directions, fails to finish things, and disrupts class discipline. Figure 5-2 shows the TRF problem items, indicating those that differ from items on the CBCL/4-16.

SCORES AND SCALES OF THE TRF

Teachers' responses are scored on the TRF Profile, which consists of scales for school performance and adaptive function-

40

CHILD BEHAVIOR CHECKLIST—TEACHER'S REPORT FORM

PUPIL'S NAME	SCHOOL

PUPIL'S AGE	PUPIL'S SEX ☐ Boy ☐ Girl	ETHNIC GROUP OR RACE	PARENTS' TYPE OF WORK *(Please be as specific as you can – for example, auto mechanic, high school teacher, homemaker, laborer, lathe operator, shoe salesman, army sergeant.)*

GRADE

THIS FORM FILLED OUT BY
☐ Teacher (name) _____
☐ Counselor (name) _____

DATE

☐ Other (specify) _____
  n a m e :

FATHER'S
TYPE OF WORK: _____

MOTHER'S
TYPE OF WORK: _____

Please try to answer each item as completely as possible, even if you lack full information.

I.   How long have you known this pupil?

II. How well do you know him/her?   ☐ Very Well   ☐ Moderately Well   ☐ Not Well

III. How much time does he/she spend in your class per week?

IV. What kind of class is it?   (Please be specific, e.g., regular 5th grade, 7th grade math, etc.)

V.   Has he/she ever been referred for special class placement, services, or tutoring?

  ☐ No   ☐ Don't Know   ☐ Yes – what kind and when?

VI. Has he/she ever repeated a grade?

  ☐ No   ☐ Don't Know   ☐ Yes – grade and reason

VII. **Current school performance** – list academic subjects and check appropriate column:

Academic subject	1. Far below grade	2. Somewhat below grade	3. At grade level	4. Somewhat above grade	5. Far above grade
1. _____	☐	☐	☐	☐	☐
2. _____	☐	☐	☐	☐	☐
3. _____	☐	☐	☐	☐	☐
4. _____	☐	☐	☐	☐	☐
5. _____	☐	☐	☐	☐	☐
6. _____	☐	☐	☐	☐	☐

Figure 5-1. Page 1 of the Teacher's Report Form.

VIII. Compared to typical pupils of the same age:	1. Much less	2. Somewhat less	3. Slightly less	4. About average	5. Slightly more	6. Somewhat more	7. Much more
1. How hard is he/she working?	☐	☐	☐	☐	☐	☐	☐
2. How appropriately is he/she behaving?	☐	☐	☐	☐	☐	☐	☐
3. How much is he/she learning?	☐	☐	☐	☐	☐	☐	☐
4. How happy is he/she?	☐	☐	☐	☐	☐	☐	☐

IX.   Most recent achievement test scores (If available):

Name of test	Subject	Date	Percentile or grade level obtained

X.   IQ, readiness, or aptitude tests (If available):

Name of test	Date	IQ or equivalent scores

XI.   Please feel free to write any comments about this pupil's work, behavior, or potential, using extra pages if necessary

_____
_____
_____
_____
_____
_____
_____
_____
_____
_____
_____
_____
_____
_____
_____
_____
_____
_____

Figure 5-1 (cont.). Page 2 of the Teacher's Report Form.

Below is a list of items that describe pupils. For each item that describes the pupil **now or within the past 2 months**, please circle the **2** if the item is **very true** or **often true** of the pupil. Circle the **1** if the item is **somewhat** or **sometimes true** of the pupil. If the item is **not true** of the pupil, circle the **0**. Please answer all items as well as you can, even if some do not seem to apply to this pupil.

0 = Not True (as far as you know)   1 = Somewhat or Sometimes True   2 = Very True or Often True

0 1 2	1. Acts too young for his/her age		0 1 2	31. Fears he/she might think or do something bad
0 1 2	a2. Hums or makes other odd noises in class		0 1 2	32. Feels he/she has to be perfect
0 1 2	3. Argues a lot		0 1 2	33. Feels or complains that no one loves him/her
0 1 2	a4. Fails to finish things he/she starts		0 1 2	34. Feels others are out to get him/her
0 1 2	5. Behaves like opposite sex		0 1 2	35. Feels worthless or inferior
0 1 2	a6. Defiant, talks back to staff		0 1 2	36. Gets hurt a lot, accident-prone
0 1 2	7. Bragging, boasting		0 1 2	37. Gets in many fights
0 1 2	8. Can't concentrate, can't pay attention for long		0 1 2	38. Gets teased a lot
0 1 2	9. Can't get his/her mind off certain thoughts; obsessions (describe):_____		0 1 2	b39. Hangs around with others who get in trouble
			0 1 2	40. Hears things that aren't there (describe):
0 1 2	10. Can't sit still, restless, or hyperactive		0 1 2	41. Impulsive or acts without thinking
			0 1 2	42. Likes to be alone
0 1 2	11. Clings to adults or too dependent			
0 1 2	12. Complains of loneliness		0 1 2	43. Lying or cheating
			0 1 2	44. Bites fingernails
0 1 2	13. Confused or seems to be in a fog			
0 1 2	14. Cries a lot		0 1 2	45. Nervous, high-strung, or tense
			0 1 2	46. Nervous movements or twitching (describe):
0 1 2	a15. Fidgets			
0 1 2	16. Cruelty, bullying, or meanness to others			
			0 1 2	a47. Overconforms to rules
0 1 2	17. Daydreams or gets lost in his/her thoughts		0 1 2	b48. Not liked by other pupils
0 1 2	18. Deliberately harms self or attempts suicide			
			0 1 2	a49. Has difficulty learning
0 1 2	19. Demands a lot of attention		0 1 2	50. Too fearful or anxious
0 1 2	20. Destroys his/her own things			
			0 1 2	51. Feels dizzy
0 1 2	b21. Destroys property belonging to others		0 1 2	52. Feels too guilty
0 1 2	a22. Difficulty following directions			
			0 1 2	a53. Talks out of turn
0 1 2	23. Disobedient at school		0 1 2	54. Overtired
0 1 2	a24. Disturbs other pupils			
			0 1 2	55. Overweight
0 1 2	b25. Doesn't get along with other pupils			56. Physical problems without known medical cause:
0 1 2	26. Doesn't seem to feel guilty after misbehaving		0 1 2	a. Aches or pains
			0 1 2	b. Headaches
0 1 2	27. Easily jealous		0 1 2	c. Nausea, feels sick
0 1 2	28. Eats or drinks things that are not food (describe): _____		0 1 2	d. Problems with eyes (describe): _____
			0 1 2	e. Rashes or other skin problems
			0 1 2	f. Stomachaches or cramps
			0 1 2	g. Vomiting, throwing up
0 1 2	29. Fears certain animals, situations, or places other than school (describe): _____		0 1 2	h. Other (describe): _____
0 1 2	30. Fears going to school			

PAGE 3   *Please see other side*

Figure 5-2. Page 3 of the Teacher's Report Form. Items marked *a* replace CBCL/4-16 items, while those marked *b* differ slightly from CBCL items.

0 = Not True			**1 = Somewhat or Sometimes True**			**2 = Very True or Often True**	

0 1 2	57. Physically attacks people	0 1 2 84. Strange behavior (describe): _____
0 1 2	58. Picks nose, skin, or other parts of body (describe): _____	
		0 1 2 85. Strange ideas (describe): _____
0 1 2 ᵃ59.	Sleeps in class	
0 1 2 ᵃ60.	Apathetic or unmotivated	0 1 2 86. Stubborn, sullen, or irritable
		0 1 2 87. Sudden changes in mood or feelings
0 1 2	61. Poor school work	0 1 2 88. Sulks a lot
0 1 2	62. Poorly coordinated or clumsy	
		0 1 2 89. Suspicious
0 1 2 ᵇ63.	Prefers being with older children	0 1 2 90. Swearing or obscene language
0 1 2 ᵇ64.	Prefers being with younger children	
		0 1 2 91. Talks about killing self
0 1 2	65. Refuses to talk	0 1 2 ᵃ92. Underachieving, not working up to potential
0 1 2	66. Repeats certain acts over and over; compulsions (describe): _____	
		0 1 2 93. Talks too much
		0 1 2 94. Teases a lot
		0 1 2 95. Temper tantrums or hot temper
0 1 2 ᵃ67.	Disrupts class discipline	0 1 2 ᵇ96. Seems preoccupied with sex
0 1 2	68. Screams a lot	
		0 1 2 97. Threatens people
0 1 2	69. Secretive, keeps things to self	0 1 2 ᵃ98. Tardy to school or class
0 1 2	70. Sees things that aren't there (describe): _____	
		0 1 2 99. Too concerned with neatness or cleanliness
		0 1 2 ᵃ100. Fails to carry out assigned tasks
		0 1 2 ᵇ101. Truancy or unexplained absence
0 1 2	71. Self-conscious or easily embarrassed	0 1 2 102. Underactive, slow moving, or lacks energy
0 1 2 ᵃ72.	Messy work	
		0 1 2 103. Unhappy, sad, or depressed
0 1 2 ᵃ73.	Behaves irresponsibly (describe): _____	0 1 2 104. Unusually loud
		0 1 2 105. Uses alcohol or drugs (describe): _____
0 1 2	74. Showing off or clowning	
		0 1 2 ᵃ106. Overly anxious to please
0 1 2	75. Shy or timid	
0 1 2 ᵃ76.	Explosive and unpredictable behavior	0 1 2 ᵃ107. Dislikes school
		0 1 2 ᵃ108. Is afraid of making mistakes
0 1 2 ᵃ77.	Demands must be met immediately, easily frustrated	
0 1 2 ᵃ78.	Inattentive, easily distracted	0 1 2 109. Whining
		0 1 2 ᵃ110. Unclean personal appearance
0 1 2	79. Speech problem (describe): _____	
		0 1 2 111. Withdrawn, doesn't get involved with others
		0 1 2 112. Worrying
0 1 2	80. Stares blankly	
		113. Please write in any problems the pupil has that were not listed above:
0 1 2 ᵃ81.	Feels hurt when criticized	
0 1 2	82. Steals	0 1 2 _____
0 1 2	83. Stores up things he/she doesn't need (describe): _____	0 1 2 _____
		0 1 2 _____

PAGE 4   *PLEASE BE SURE YOU HAVE ANSWERED ALL ITEMS*

Figure 5-2 (cont.). Page 4 of the Teacher's Report Form. Items marked *a* replace CBCL/4-16 items, while those marked *b* differ slightly from CBCL items.

ing as well as empirically-derived problem scales. Table 5-1 summarizes the scales of the TRF, including the narrow-band syndrome scales derived from factor analyses of TRFs completed for 1,700 clinically-referred children and normed on 1,100 nonreferred children. The scoring profiles are standardized separately for each sex in the age ranges shown in Table 5-1. The *Manual for the Teacher's Report Form* (Achenbach & Edelbrock, 1986) provides detailed information on scoring procedures for the TRF, as well as reliability, validity, standardization samples, and other information on its development and applications.

Adaptive Functioning Scales

Figure 5-3 shows the hand-scored version of the TRF scales for school performance and adaptive functioning for Michael, the 11-year-old boy discussed in Chapter 3, while Table 5-2 provides an explanation of each score on the profile. The procedures for hand scoring adaptive functioning are described in the *Manual* for the TRF. Michael's score of 7 for total adaptive functioning was in the clinical range compared to norms for boys aged 6-11 ($T = 30$; <13th percentile). His teacher rated him below the typical pupil on school performance, working hard, behaving appropriately, learning, and happiness.

Problem Scales

Figure 5-4 shows the hand-scored version of the TRF problem scales for 11-year-old Michael. The types of scores obtained are the same as those described in Chapter 3 for the hand-scored version of the problem scales of the CBCL/4-16, with the minor exception of a difference in the percentiles for clinical cutoffs. The 89th percentile on the TRF total problem, Internalizing, and Externalizing scales serves as the clinical cutoff between the normal and clinical range, because it was found to discriminate better between nonreferred children and children referred for special school or mental health services

Table 5-1
Scales Scored from the Teacher's Report Form[a]

School Performance	Total Problems
Total Adaptive Functioning	Internalizing
Working hard	Externalizing
Behaving appropriately	
Learning	
Happy	

Narrow-Band Syndromes

Boys 6-11	*Girls 6-11*
Anxious	Anxious
Social Withdrawal	Social Withdrawal
Unpopular	Depressed
Self-Destructive	Unpopular
Obsessive-Compulsive	Self-Destructive
Inattentive	Inattentive
Nervous-Overactive	Nervous-Overactive
Aggressive	Aggressive

Boys 12-16	*Girls 12-16*
Social Withdrawal	Anxious
Anxious	Social Withdrawal
Unpopular	Depressed
Obsessive-Compulsive	Immature
Immature	Self-Destructive
Self-Destructive	Inattentive
Inattentive	Unpopular
Aggressive	Delinquent
	Aggressive

[a]Scales were derived from teachers' ratings of 1,700 clinically-referred children and normed on 1,100 nonreferred children.

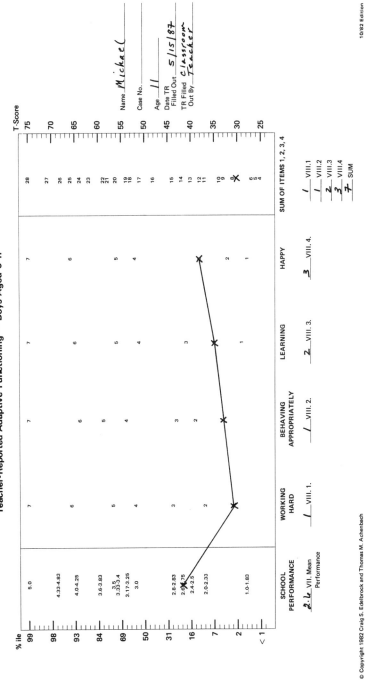

The Child Behavior Profile — Teacher's Report Version

Teacher-Reported Adaptive Functioning — Boys Aged 6-11

Figure 5-3. Hand-scored version of TRF adaptive functioning scales for 11-year-old Michael. Note that there is a clinical cutoff at the 13th percentile only for the total adaptive functioning score.

than the 90th percentile used on the CBCL/4-16. Like the CBCL/4-16, however, the 98th percentile is the clinical cutoff for the TRF narrow-band scales. Scores on the problem scales are explained in Chapter 3.

Table 5-2
Explanations of Scores on the Adaptive Functioning Scales of the TRF Profile

---

Percentiles: the percent of children in the normative sample of nonreferred children who obtained a score less than or equal to each raw score.

Raw scores: score for the teacher's ratings on school performance and adaptive functioning. The raw score for school performance is the mean of the ratings from *1* (far below grade level) to *5* (far above grade level) on each academic subject listed. Raw scores for working hard, behaving appropriately, learning, and happy are the teacher's ratings from *1* (much less) to *7* (much more), comparing the child to typical pupils of the same age. There are no clinical cutoffs for ratings of school performance, working hard, behaving appropriately, learning, or happy, though low scores indicate poor functioning.

T **scores:** standard scores based on the percentiles of raw scores for normative samples of nonreferred children. The normalized *T* scores have means near 50 and standard deviations near 10, but these vary among scales, because of skewed distributions of raw scores.

Sum of items 1, 2, 3, 4: raw score for total adaptive functioning obtained by summing the raw scores for working hard, behaving appropriately, learning, and happy. Scores below the 13th percentile are considered to be in the clinical range.

Sum *T* score: normalized *T* score for total adaptive functioning based on the normative sample of nonreferred children.

In the profile shown in Figure 5-4, Michael's total problem score of 79 was in the clinical range compared to norms for boys aged 6-11 (*T* score = 68; >89th percentile), as were his Internalizing (*T* score = 60; >89th percentile) and Externalizing scores (*T* score = 69; >89th percentile). Michael's score of 46

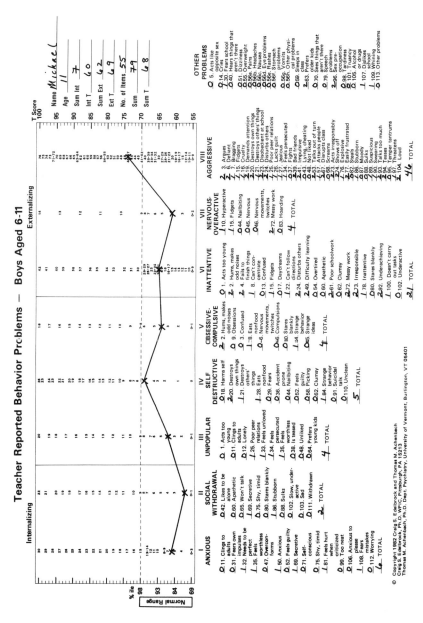

Figure 5-4. Hand-scored version of the TRF problem scales for 11-year-old Michael. Note that the clinical cutoff is the 89th percentile for the total problem score and the 98th percentile for the narrow-band scales.

on the Aggressive scale was in the clinical range (T score = 74; >98th percentile), but all his other narrow-band scale scores were in the normal range. On the Aggressive scale, Michael's teacher scored him on items such as *3. Argues a lot*; *20. Destroys his own things*; *21. Destroys property belonging to others*; *23. Disobedient at school*; *53. Talks out of turn*; *57. Physically attacks people*; *67. Disrupts class discipline*; *97. Threatens people*; and *104. Unusually loud.* Although Michael's score on the Self-Destructive scale was in the normal range, it was near the clinical cutoff due to his destruction of property. However, his teacher did not report problems relating to suicidal thoughts or behavior.

Summary of Cutoffs

Table 5-3 summarizes the cutoffs between the normal and clinical range on the TRF scales. Cutoffs are listed in terms of raw scores and percentiles for the TRF total adaptive functioning and total problem scores for each sex/age group. Cutoffs for the Internalizing, Externalizing, and narrow-band scales are given only in T scores and percentiles for all groups, since raw score cutoffs vary across these scales. As with the CBCL/4-16, clinical cutoffs on the narrow-band scales are set at a more extreme level (98th percentile) than for total problems, Internalizing, and Externalizing, because of the smaller number of items comprising each narrow-band scale.

MULTIAXIAL EMPIRICALLY-BASED ASSESS-MENT INITIATED WITH THE TRF

To provide an overview of multiaxial empirically-based assessment initiated with the TRF, Figure 5-5 illustrates a typical sequence that might occur when a teacher is the first informant. Teachers are often the first informants in school-based assessments, such as referrals for special education services or referrals to a school psychologist. In these instances, data gathering

Table 5-3
Clinical Cutoff Points for TRF Scales

Scale	Group	Raw Score	T Score	Percentile
School Performance	All groups	No clinical cutoffs		
Total Adaptive Functioning[a]	Boys 6-11	13	c	13
	Boys 12-16	11	c	13
	Girls 6-11	15	c	13
	Girls 12-16	13	c	13
Working hard, Behaving appropriately, Learning, Happy	All groups	No clinical cutoffs		
Total Problems[b]	Boys 6-11	49	c	89
	Boys 12-16	56	c	89
	Girls 6-11	38	c	89
	Girls 12-16	42	c	89
Internalizing, Externalizing[b]	All groups	Varies	63	89
Narrow-band Syndromes[b]	All groups	Varies	70	98

[a]Scores *below* the cutoffs are in the clinical range.
[b]Scores *above* the cutoffs are in the clinical range.
[c]The raw score, not the T score, is used as the clinical cutoff on this scale, since more than one raw score corresponds to the same T score for some groups.

can begin with the TRF after the practitioner receives the initial referral complaints from the teacher. If the child has more than one teacher, it is helpful to obtain TRFs from all available teachers. The TRF scores then enable the practitioner to determine whether the reported problems deviate from norms for non-referred agemates of the same sex. A review of the child's educational record can provide historical data to determine whether problems were evident in the past and whether there are any additional concerns. An interview with the teacher

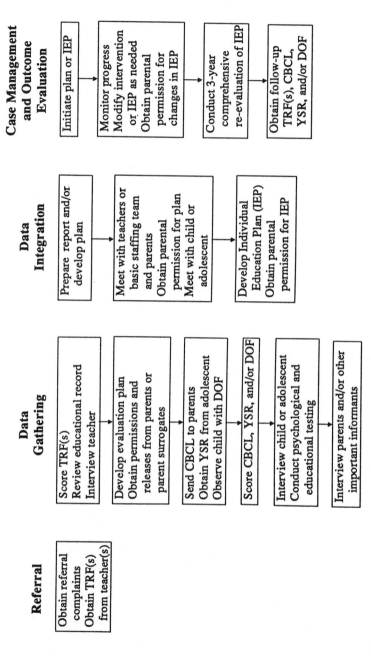

Figure 5-5. Illustrative sequence of empirically-based assessment where the teacher is the first informant.

should be used to obtain further details of the child's current achievement and problems reported on the TRF. If scores on the TRF are all well in the normal range and there are no problems with school achievement, this may argue against more extensive evaluation. Scores on individual items of the TRF can, however, highlight specific problems that would require intervention, such as failing to complete assignments, disturbing other children, or difficulty concentrating. If TRF scores are in the clinical range and/or the child's school achievement is below the level expected from ability measures, then further assessment is usually warranted.

After initial data gathering, the practitioner develops an evaluation plan in consultation with the teacher or as part of a basic staffing team and obtains appropriate permissions and releases from the parents. Federal and state regulations stipulate specific procedures for special education assessments that can easily incorporate the TRF and other empirically-based measures. For most cases concerning school problems, it is desirable to obtain information from the parents concerning the child's functioning. Sending the CBCL to the parents provides an economical and efficient way of gaining their perspective on competencies and problems. The purpose of the CBCL should be explained by phone or letter, however, to prepare parents for questions about behavioral/emotional problems. For adolescents 11 through 18, the YSR can also be used to obtain their perspective on their own competencies and problems. In the school setting, it is particularly important that the adolescent be provided a private place to complete the YSR and that all responses be kept strictly confidential, as should other assessment results. Classroom observations with the DOF can also provide a more direct sampling of behavior to compare with the teacher's, parent's, and self ratings. Many states require such observations as part of their special education assessment procedures. We recommend averaging DOF scores over at least three 10-minute observations made on separate days, since problem behavior is apt to vary from day to day. Further details of the YSR and DOF are presented in Chapters 6 and 7.

TRF and CBCL findings can be addressed in interviews with children and adolescents. Interviews with adolescents can also focus on responses to the YSR, as well as their opinions about teachers' and parents' reports of problems. Interviews with younger children might focus on findings from the direct observations in the classroom, as well as on reports from teachers and parents. Other aspects of the interview can cover personal issues, attitudes, motivation toward school, and teaching and behavior management strategies that might be helpful to the child. Psychological and educational testing may either precede or follow the interview and should address the initial referral complaints and other problems identified with the empirically-based measures. Interviews with parents and/or other important informants, such as guidance counselors or case workers, can be used to clarify written responses and to pursue special concerns.

Once the evaluation is complete, the data must be integrated to form a comprehensive picture of the child's current functioning and needs. In special education assessments, this takes the form of a written report. Evaluations by school psychologists usually culminate in a written report. These reports may have their own special formats or may be modeled on the examples presented in Chapter 8. For school reports, it is usually appropriate to summarize the TRF, CBCL, YSR, and DOF results in a general way without specifying scores or scale names. The various profiles can be compared to identify variations in the child's functioning in different classes or at home versus school. Such comparisons can give important clues about what type of classes, teaching styles, or general educational environments enhance the child's adaptive functioning and behavior. Elsewhere, we have described ways in which information on the CBCL, TRF, YSR, and DOF can be used to determine whether a child meets federal criteria for serious emotional disturbance according to Public Law 94-142 (see Achenbach & Edelbrock, 1987; Achenbach & McConaughy, 1987; McConaughy & Achenbach,1988).

The written report should also outline a plan for addressing the educational and behavioral/emotional needs identified in the evaluation. In most school-based assessments, the practitioner meets with the teachers or basic staffing team to develop such a plan. At least one meeting usually includes the parents as well, in order to obtain their permission for interventions. It is also appropriate to have a special meeting with the child to explain the findings of the evaluation and gain his/her cooperation in the interventions. This is particularly helpful for older children and adolescents in order to allay any fears or misconceptions about the evaluation and to enhance their motivation for change. In special education assessments, an additional step involves the writing of the Individual Education Plan (IEP). This is usually done by the basic staffing team and requires signatures from parents indicating their agreement. Information from the TRF and other measures can be used to develop interventions addressing competencies and behavioral/emotional problems in school. Some school districts have carried this even further by utilizing CBCL and TRF items to define behavioral objectives for an Individual Education and Therapeutic Plan (IETP) for seriously emotionally disturbed children.

Once the plan has been initiated, it is important to monitor the child's progress and modify interventions as needed. In the school setting, the child's learning is commonly measured with periodic achievement testing. Adaptive functioning and behavior problems can also be monitored by obtaining the TRF from teachers at regular intervals, such as 2, 4, or 6 months, or the end of each marking period. Comparing TRF profiles across intervals provides a comprehensive picture of changes in behavior. If desired improvements have not occurred, it may be necessary to modify the intervention and obtain parental permission for changes in the IEP. For special education cases, a comprehensive re-evaluation is required every 3 years. The re-evaluation should include the TRF and any other empirically-based measures used in the initial evaluation. This will allow comparisons of the child's competencies and behavior across the 3-year period, as well as comparisons of academic achievement and ability. The 3-year re-evaluation is one form of follow-up and outcome assessment built into special education regulations. Follow-up evaluations with the TRF, CBCL, YSR, and/or DOF are also recommended for measuring outcomes over 6- or 12-month intervals.

SUMMARY

The TRF is designed to obtain teachers' reports of their pupils' school performance, adaptive functioning, and behavioral/emotional problems. Teachers' responses are scored on the scales of the TRF Profile, which is standardized separately for each sex at ages 6-11 and 12-16. The scales are listed in Table 5-1, while cutoffs for distinguishing between the normal and clinical ranges are summarized in Table 5-3. Figure 5-5 illustrates a typical sequence of multiaxial empirically-based assessment initiated with the TRF.

Chapter 6
The Youth Self-Report (YSR)

The YSR (buff form) is a four-page form designed to obtain self-reports of social competence and behavioral/emotional problems from 11- to 18-year-olds. It requires a mental age of at least 10 years and fifth grade reading skills, but it can be read aloud to those with reading skills below fifth grade. Figures 6-1 and 6-2 show that the YSR has most of the same competence and problem items as the CBCL/4-16, but the items are stated in the first person. Sixteen CBCL problem items considered inappropriate to ask adolescents were replaced with 16 socially desirable items that enable respondents to report something favorable about themselves. The favorable items are omitted from the total problem score. Respondents rate themselves on 103 problem items using a 0-1-2 scale for how true the item is now or within the past 6 months. The respondent circles a 2 if the item is *very true or often true*; *1* if the item is *somewhat or sometimes true*; or *0* if the item is *not true*. All 103 problem items correspond to those on the CBCL/4-16 and 90 correspond to those on the TRF. Figure 6-2 indicates the YSR problem items that differ from those on the CBCL/4-16 and TRF.

SCORES AND SCALES OF THE YSR

YSR responses are scored on the YSR Profile, which consists of Activities and Social scales like those on the CBCL/4-16 Profile, a score for school performance, a total competence score, and empirically-derived problem scales, plus scores for Internalizing, Externalizing, and total problems. Table 6-1 lists the scales of the YSR, including the narrow-band syndromes derived from factor analyses of YSRs completed by 927 clinically-referred youths and normed on 686 nonreferred

57

YOUTH SELF-REPORT FOR AGES 11–18

YOUR AGE	YOUR SEX ☐ Boy ☐ Girl	GRADE IN SCHOOL	YOUR NAME

| YOUR RACE
☐ Black
☐ White
☐ Other (specify) | TODAY'S DATE
Mo. _____ Date _____ Yr. _____

DATE OF BIRTH
Mo. _____ Date _____ Yr. _____ | PARENT'S TYPE OF WORK *(Please be specific—for example: auto mechanic, high school teacher, homemaker, laborer, lathe operator, shoe salesman, army sergeant.)*
FATHER'S
TYPE OF WORK: _____
MOTHER'S
TYPE OF WORK: _____ |

I. Please list the sports you most like to take part in. For example: swimming, baseball, skating, skate boarding, bike riding, fishing, etc.

☐ None

Compared to others of your age, about how much time do you spend in each?

Compared to others of your age, how well do you do each one?

	Less Than Average	Average	More Than Average		Below Average	Average	Above Average
a. _____	☐	☐	☐		☐	☐	☐
b. _____	☐	☐	☐		☐	☐	☐
c. _____	☐	☐	☐		☐	☐	☐

II. Please list your favorite hobbies, activities, and games, other than sports. For example: cards, books, piano, crafts, etc. (Do not include T.V.)

☐ None

Compared to others of your age, about how much time do you spend in each?

Compared to others of your age, how well do you do each one?

	Less Than Average	Average	More Than Average		Below Average	Average	Above Average
a. _____	☐	☐	☐		☐	☐	☐
b. _____	☐	☐	☐		☐	☐	☐
c. _____	☐	☐	☐		☐	☐	☐

III. Please list any organization, clubs, teams or groups you belong to.

☐ None

Compared to others of your age, how active are you in each?

	Less Active	Average	More Active
a. _____	☐	☐	☐
b. _____	☐	☐	☐
c. _____	☐	☐	☐

IV. Please list any jobs or chores you have. For example: Paper route, babysitting, making bed, etc.

☐ None

Compared to others of your age, how well do you carry them out?

	Below Average	Average	Above Average
a. _____	☐	☐	☐
b. _____	☐	☐	☐
c. _____	☐	☐	☐

Figure 6-1. Competence items on Page 1 of the Youth Self-Report.

V. **1. About how many close friends do you have?** ☐ None ☐ 1 ☐ 2 or 3 ☐ 4 or more

2. About how many times a week do you do things with them? ☐ less than 1 ☐ 1 or 2 ☐ 3 or more

VI. **Compared to others of your age, how well do you:**

	Worse	About the same	Better
a. Get along with your brothers & sisters?	☐	☐	☐
b. Get along with other kids?	☐	☐	☐
c. Get along with your parents?	☐	☐	☐
d. Do things by yourself?	☐	☐	☐

VII. **Current school performance**

☐ I do not go to school

		Failing	Below Average	Average	Above Average
	a. English	☐	☐	☐	☐
	b. Math	☐	☐	☐	☐
Other subjects:	c. _____	☐	☐	☐	☐
	d. _____	☐	☐	☐	☐
	e. _____	☐	☐	☐	☐
	f. _____	☐	☐	☐	☐
	g. _____	☐	☐	☐	☐

Please describe any concerns or problems you have about school

Figure 6-1(cont.). Competence items on Page 2 of the Youth Self-Report

VIII. Below is a list of items that describe kids. For each item that describes you **now** or **within the past 6 months**, please circle the 2 if the item is **very true** or **often true** of you. Circle the 1 if the item is **somewhat** or **sometimes true** of you. If the item is **not true** of you, circle the 0.

0 = Not True   1 = Somewhat or Sometimes True   2 = Very True or Often True

CBCL   TRF

0 1 2   1. I act too young for my age
0 1 2   2. I have an allergy (describe): ^{c} _____

_____

0 1 2   3. I argue a lot
0 1 2   4. I have asthma ^{c}
0 1 2   5. I act like the opposite sex
0 1 2 ^{a} 6. I like animals ^{c}
0 1 2 ^{b} 7. I brag ^{d}
0 1 2   8. I have trouble concentrating^{d} or paying attention
0 1 2   9. I can't get my mind off certain ^{d} thoughts (describe): _____

_____

0 1 2 ^{b} 10. I have trouble sitting still ^{d}
0 1 2 ^{b} 11. I'm too dependent on adults ^{d}
0 1 2   12. I feel lonely
0 1 2   13. I feel confused or in a fog
0 1 2   14. I cry a lot
0 1 2 ^{a} 15. I am pretty honest ^{c}
0 1 2   16. I am mean to others ^{d}
0 1 2   17. I daydream a lot ^{d}
0 1 2   18. I deliberately try to hurt or kill myself
0 1 2 ^{b} 19. I try to get a lot of attention ^{d}
0 1 2   20. I destroy my things
0 1 2   21. I destroy things belonging to others
0 1 2   22. I disobey my parents ^{c}
0 1 2   23. I disobey at school
0 1 2   24. I don't eat as well as I should ^{c}
0 1 2   25. I don't get along with other kids
0 1 2   26. I don't feel guilty after doing ^{d} something I shouldn't
0 1 2   27. I am jealous of others
0 1 2 ^{a} 28. I am willing to help others ^{c} when they need help
0 1 2   29. I am afraid of certain animals, situations, or places, other than school (describe): _____

_____

0 1 2   30. I am afraid of going to school
0 1 2   31. I am afraid I might think or do something bad
0 1 2   32. I feel that I have to be perfect
0 1 2   33. I feel that no one loves me
0 1 2   34. I feel that others are out to get me
0 1 2   35. I feel worthless or inferior
0 1 2   36. I accidentally get hurt a lot ^{d}
0 1 2   37. I get in many fights
0 1 2   38. I get teased a lot
0 1 2   39. I hang around with kids who get in trouble

CBCL   TRF

0 1 2   40. I hear things that nobody else seems able to hear (describe): ^{d} _____

_____

0 1 2 ^{b}41. I act without stopping to think ^{d}
0 1 2   42. I like to be alone
0 1 2   43. I lie or cheat
0 1 2   44. I bite my fingernails
0 1 2   45. I am nervous or tense ^{d}
0 1 2   46. Parts of my body twitch or make nervous movements (describe):

_____

_____

0 1 2   47. I have nightmares ^{c}
0 1 2   48. I am not liked by other kids
0 1 2 ^{a}49. I can do certain things better ^{c} than most kids
0 1 2   50. I am too fearful or anxious
0 1 2   51. I feel dizzy
0 1 2   52. I feel too guilty
0 1 2   53. I eat too much ^{c}
0 1 2   54. I feel overtired
0 1 2   55. I am overweight
     56. Physical problems without known medical cause:
0 1 2   a. Aches or pains
0 1 2   b. Headaches
0 1 2   c. Nausea, feel sick
0 1 2   d. Problems with eyes (describe):

_____

_____

0 1 2   e. Rashes or other skin problems
0 1 2   f. Stomachaches or cramps
0 1 2   g. Vomiting, throwing up
0 1 2   h. Other (describe): _____

_____

0 1 2   57. I physically attack people
0 1 2 ^{b}58. I pick my skin or other parts ^{d} of my body (describe):_____

_____

0 1 2 ^{a} 59. I can be pretty friendly ^{c}
0 1 2 ^{a} 60. I like to try new things ^{c}
0 1 2   61. My school work is poor
0 1 2   62. I am poorly coordinated or clumsy
0 1 2   63. I would rather be with older ^{d} kids than with kids my own age

Figure 6-2. Problem items on Page 3 of the Youth Self-Report. Superscripts to the *left* of items: *a* indicates socially desirable items that replace *CBCL* items, while *b* indicates items that differ slightly from *CBCL* items. Superscripts to the *right* of items: *c* indicates that the item has no direct counterpart on the *TRF*, while *d* indicates that it differs slightly from the *TRF*.

0 = Not True   1 = Somewhat or Sometimes True   2 = Very True or Often True

CBCL				TRF
0	1	2	64. I would rather be with younger kids than with kids my own age d	
0	1	2	65. I refuse to talk	
0	1	2	66. I repeat certain actions over and over (describe): _____ d	
0	1	2	67. I run away from home C	
0	1	2	68. I scream a lot	
0	1	2	69. I am secretive or keep things to myself	
0	1	2	70. I see things that nobody else seems able to see (describe): _____ d	
0	1	2	71. I am self-conscious or easily embarrassed	
0	1	2	72. I set fires C	
0	1	2 a	73. I can work well with my hands C	
0	1	2	74. I show off or clown	
0	1	2	75. I am shy d	
0	1	2	76. I sleep less than most kids C	
0	1	2	77. I sleep more than most kids C during day and/or night (describe): _____	
0	1	2 a	78. I have a good imagination C	
0	1	2	79. I have a speech problem (describe): _____	
0	1	2 a	80. I stand up for my rights C	
0	1	2	81. I steal things at home C	
0	1	2	82. I steal things from places other than home	
0	1	2	83. I store up things I don't need (describe): _____	
0	1	2	84. I do things other people think are strange (describe): _____ d	

CBCL				TRF
0	1	2	85. I have thoughts that other people would think are strange d (describe): _____	
0	1	2 b	86. I am stubborn d	
0	1	2	87. My moods or feelings change suddenly	
0	1	2 a	88. I enjoy being with other people C	
0	1	2	89. I am suspicious	
0	1	2	90. I swear or use dirty language	
0	1	2	91. I think about killing myself d	
0	1	2 a	92. I like to make others laugh C	
0	1	2	93. I talk too much	
0	1	2	94. I tease others a lot	
0	1	2	95. I have a hot temper d	
0	1	2	96. I think about sex too much	
0	1	2	97. I threaten to hurt people	
0	1	2 a	98. I like to help others C	
0	1	2	99. I am too concerned about being neat or clean	
0	1	2	100. I have trouble sleeping (describe): C _____	
0	1	2	101. I cut classes or skip school	
0	1	2 b	102. I don't have much energy d	
0	1	2	103. I am unhappy, sad, or depressed	
0	1	2	104. I am louder than other kids	
0	1	2	105. I use alcohol or drugs other than for medical conditions (describe): _____	
0	1	2 a	106. I try to be fair to others C	
0	1	2 a	107. I enjoy a good joke C	
0	1	2 a	108. I like to take life easy C	
0	1	2 a	109. I try to help other people when I can C	
0	1	2	110. I wish I were of the opposite sex C	
0	1	2	111. I keep from getting involved with others d	
0	1	2	112. I worry a lot	

Please write down anything else that describes your feelings, behavior, or interests

Figure 6-2 (cont.). Problem items on Page 4 of the Youth Self-Report. Superscripts to the *left* of items: *a* indicates socially desirable items that replace *CBCL* items, while *b* indicates items that differ slightly from *CBCL* items. Superscripts to the *right* of items: *c* indicates that the item has no direct counterpart on the *TRF*, while *d* indicates that it differs slightly from the *TRF*.

youths. The scoring profiles for the YSR are standardized separately for each sex at ages 11-18. The *Manual for the Youth Self-Report* (Achenbach & Edelbrock, 1987) provides detailed information on scoring procedures, as well as data on reliability, validity, standardization samples, and other information on its development and applications.

Table 6-1
Scales Scored from the Youth Self-Report[a]

Total Competence	Total Problems
Activities	Internalizing
Social	Externalizing

Narrow-Band Syndromes

Boys 11-18	*Girls 11-18*
Depressed	Somatic Complaints
Unpopular	Depressed
Somatic Complaints	Unpopular
Self Destructive/	Thought Disorder
Identity Problems	Aggressive
Thought Disorder	Delinquent
Delinquent	
Aggressive	

[a]Scales were derived from self-ratings by 927 clinically-referred youths and 686 nonreferred youths.

Competence Scales

Figure 6-3 shows the hand-scored profile of the Activities and Social scales of the YSR completed by Michael, the 11-year-old boy discussed in Chapters 3 and 5. A mean score is also computed for the self-ratings of academic subjects, from failing (scored *0*) to above average (scored *3*), rounded to the nearest *.5*. The school performance score does not constitute a separate scale, but is included in the total competence score. As

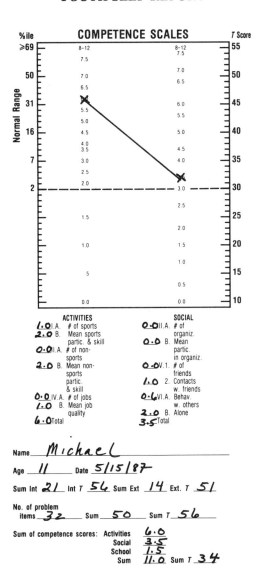

COMPETENCE SCALES

%ile

≥69

50

31

16

7

2

Normal Range

T Score

55

50

45

40

35

30

25

20

15

10

ACTIVITIES

1.0 I.A. # of sports
2.0 B. Mean sports
partic. & skill
0.0 I.A. # of non-
sports
2.0 B. Mean non-
sports
partic.
& skill
0.0 IV.A. # of jobs
1.0 B. Mean job
quality
6.0 Total

SOCIAL

0.0 II.A. # of
organiz.
0.0 B. Mean
partic.
in organiz.
0.0 V.1. # of
friends
1.0 2. Contacts
w. friends
0.6 VI.A. Behav.
w. others
2.0 B. Alone
3.5 Total

Name _Michael_

Age _11_ Date _5/15/87_

Sum Int _21_ Int *T* _56_ Sum Ext _14_ Ext. *T* _51_

No. of problem
items _32_ Sum _50_ Sum *T* _56_

Sum of competence scores: Activities _6.0_
Social _3.5_
School _1.5_
Sum _11.0_ Sum *T* _34_

Figure 6-3. Hand-scored version of the YSR competence scales for 11-year-old Michael. On the hand-scored YSR profile, the competence and problem scales are all shown on the same page. Note that the 2nd percentile serves as the clinical cutoff for the competence scales, but there is no cutoff for the total compteence score.

on the CBCL/4-16, the 2nd percentile serves as the clinical cutoff for the Activities and Social scales, but there is no cutoff for the YSR total competence score, because the competence score does not discriminate well between clinically-referred and nonreferred youth.

Michael's score of 6.0 on the Activities scale was in the normal range (*T* score = 46; >2nd percentile). His score of 3.5 on the Social scale was also in the normal range but close to the clinical cutoff (*T* score = 32; >2nd percentile). Although there are no clinical cutoffs for the total competence score, comparison with mean scores provided in the YSR *Manual* showed that Michael's score of 11.0 was below the average score of 16.8 for nonreferred boys aged 11-18.

Problem Scales

Figure 6-4 shows the hand-scored version of the YSR problem scales for 11-year-old Michael. The scores for total problems, Internalizing, and Externalizing are shown near the bottom of Figure 6-3. The types of scores obtained are the same as those described in Chapter 3 for the hand-scored version of the problem scales of the CBCL/4-16, with the minor exception that the 89th percentile serves as the clinical cutoff on the YSR total problem, Internalizing, and Externalizing scores. As on the CBCL/4-16 and TRF, the 98th percentile serves as the clinical cutoff for the YSR narrow-band scales. Chapter 3 explains the types of scores derived from the problem scales. Note that the 16 socially desirable items are excluded when computing the YSR total problem score.

Although Michael acknowledged a number of problems, his total problem score of 50 was in the normal range for boys aged 11-18 (*T* score = 56; <89th percentile). His Internalizing score of 21 was also in the normal range (*T* score = 56; <89th percentile), as was his Externalizing score of 14 (*T* score = 51; <89th percentile). Michael's highest scores were on the Unpopular scale (*T* score = 65), including items such as *14. I cry a lot ; 31. I am afraid I might think or do something bad; 33. I feel that no*

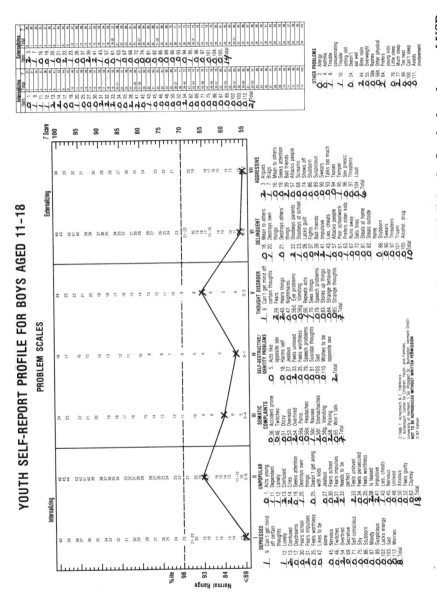

Figure 6-4. Hand-scored version of the YSR problem scales for 11-year-old Michael. On the hand-scored YSR profile, the Internalizing and Externalizing scores are listed under the competence scales as shown in Figure 6-3. Note that the clinical cutoff is the 89th percentile for the total problem score and the 98th percentile for the narrow-band scales.

one loves me; and *38. I get teased a lot*; and on the Thought Disorder scale (*T* score = 65), including items such as *29. I am afraid of certain animals, situations, or places, other than school*; *40. I hear things that nobody else seems able to hear*; and *70. I see things that nobody else seems able to see.* Michael noted that he hears funny noises at night for item 40, but did not indicate what strange things he sees on item 70.

Summary of Cutoffs

Table 6-2 summarizes the clinical cutoffs for the YSR competence and problem scales. Cutoffs are listed in terms of raw scores and percentiles for the total problem score for both sexes. Cutoffs for the competence scales, Internalizing, Externalizing, and narrow-band problem scales are given only in terms of *T* scores and percentiles, since raw score cutoffs vary across these scales. There is no cutoff for the total competence score.

Table 6-2
Clinical Cutoff Points for YSR Scales

Scale	*Group*	*Raw Score*	*T Score*	*Percentile*
Total Competence	Both sexes	No clinical cutoffs		
Activities, School[a]	Both sexes	Varies	30	2
Total Problems[b]	Boys 11-18	68	c	89
	Girls 11-18	70	c	89
Internalizing, Externalizing[b]	Both sexes	Varies	62	89
Narrow-band Syndromes[b]	Both sexes	Varies	70	98

[a]Scores *below* the cutoffs are in the clinical range.
[b]Scores *above* the cutoffs are in the clinical range.
[c]The raw score, not the *T* score, is used as the clinical cutoff on this scale, since more than one raw score corresponds to the same *T* score.

MULTIAXIAL EMPIRICALLY-BASED ASSESS-MENT INITIATED WITH THE YSR

To provide an overview of multiaxial empirically-based assessment initiated with the YSR, Figure 6-5 illustrates a typical sequence that might occur when an adolescent is the first informant. Self-referrals by adolescents are less common than parent or teacher referrals, but adolescents occasionally seek help from crisis clinics, teen centers, school guidance counselors, and school psychologists. In these cases, the practitioner begins by interviewing the youth about concerns that prompted the request for help. The youth can then be given the YSR in order to obtain his/her perspective on competencies and a variety of problems. If YSR scores are in the normal range, the practitioner may then discuss with the youth any problems noted on individual YSR items. If YSR scores are in the clinical range and/or responses to specific items cause alarm, then the practitioner may want further evaluation and the youth's permission to contact other important informants, such as parents and teachers. In some cases, contacting other informants is mandatory, as when the youth has indicated suicidal tendencies, behaviors that pose a danger to others, or when there is a suggestion of markedly deviant thoughts, feelings, or behaviors. Requesting CBCLs from parents and TRFs from teachers provides a way for the practitioner to initiate contacts with these other parties and to explain what prompted the youth's self-referral. Parental permission will probably be necessary for any further evaluation at this point.

Selected findings from the YSR, CBCL, and TRF can then be discussed with the youth in further interview sessions. Comparisons of the various profiles will enable the practitioner to determine whether problems reported by the youth have also been observed by parents and teachers, and whether there are any variations in problems across different settings. Psychological and educational testing may be necessary to explore learning and/or emotional problems further, and the practitioner may want to interview parents, teachers, and/or other

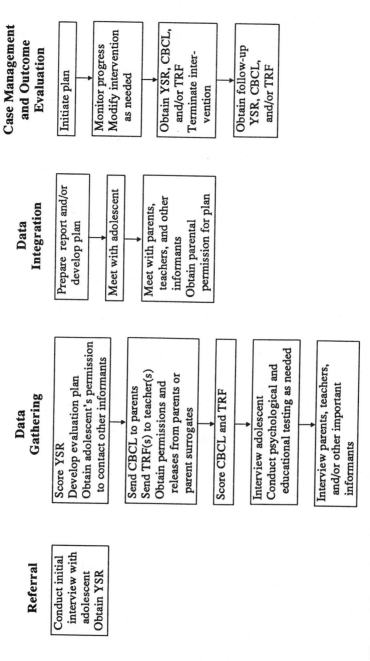

Figure 6-5. Illustrative sequence of empirically-based assessment where an adolescent is the first informant.

important informants, such as case workers or peers. To protect confidentiality and maintain the youth's trust, however, it is important that the practitioner explain the purpose of contacts with other parties, describe what will be discussed, and, preferably, obtain the youth's agreement for such contacts.

Once all the data have been gathered, the practitioner must integrate the findings to form a plan of action. Data integration may take the form of a written summary in some cases or move directly to a plan without a written report. Comprehensive clinical evaluations would result when the youth and his/her parents are referred for more extensive work-ups than usually occur in a crisis clinic, teen center, or school guidance office. Chapter 8 presents several examples of reports combining results of the YSR, CBCL, and TRF with findings from other measures. Once a plan is developed, the practitioner meets with the youth to explain the interventions and obtain his/her cooperation. A separate or joint meeting with parents, teachers, and/or other informants may also be appropriate. After a plan has been initiated, the YSR and other empirically-based measures can be used to monitor progress and determine whether interventions need to be modified. By periodically repeating the YSR and other measures obtained in the initial assessment, the practitioner can determine when it is appropriate to terminate an intervention. Follow-up evaluations with the YSR, CBCL, and TRF can then be obtained at later dates to determine whether the interventions have been effective or whether additional interventions are needed.

SUMMARY

The YSR is designed to obtain self-reports of social competence and behavioral/emotional problems from 11- to 18-year-olds. It has many of the same items as the CBCL/4-16, but they are stated in the first person. The responses are scored on the scales of the YSR Profile, which includes competence and problem scales standardized separately for each sex. The scale names are listed in Table 6-1, while cutoffs for distinguishing between the normal and clinical ranges are summarized in Table 6-2. Figure 6-5 illustrates a typical sequence of multiaxial empirically-based assessment initiated with the YSR.

Chapter 7
The Direct Observation Form (DOF)

The DOF (yellow form) is a four-page form designed for recording behavior problems observed over 10-minute intervals. The observer writes a narrative description of the child's behavior and interactions over the 10 minutes, keeping the items to be rated in view and then making the actual ratings at the end of the observation session. There are 96 specific problem items and an open-ended item on the DOF. Seventy-two of the specific items have counterparts on the CBCL and 85 on the TRF. Each item is rated on a 0-1-2-3 scale. The inclusion of one more point on the DOF scale than on the 0-1-2 scales of the other instruments allows a rating for *a very slight or ambiguous occurrence* of a behavior (scored *1*), as well as *a definite occurrence with mild to moderate intensity and less than three minutes duration* (scored *2*), and *a definite occurrence with severe intensity or greater than three minutes duration* (scored *3*). A total behavior problem score is computed by summing the scores on all 96 specific items and the open-ended item. An on-task score is also computed by summing ratings of on-task behavior during the last 5 seconds of each one-minute interval. Figure 7-1 shows the problem items and on-task ratings of the DOF, indicating problem items that differ from the CBCL and TRF. Reliability and validity data have been reported by Achenbach and Edelbrock (1983), McConaughy, Achenbach, and Gent (1988), and Reed and Edelbrock (1983).

TRAINING AND USE

Elaborate training is not required for using the DOF, but observers should be thoroughly familiar with all the items and should practice making the narrative descriptions, scoring the

DIRECT OBSERVATION FORM

For each item that describes the child's behavior **during the observational period,** circle the

- 0 if the item was not observed
- 1 if there was a very slight or ambiguous occurrence
- 2 if there was a definite occurrence with mild to moderate intensity **and** less than three minutes duration
- 3 if there was a definite occurrence with severe intensity **or** greater than three minutes duration

I = item scored on Internalizing scale
E = item scored on Externalizing scale

For each problem observed, score only the item that most specifically describes the behavior. Circle a score for every item.

CBCL/4-16   TRF   CBCL/4-16   TRF

I	0 1 2 3	b 1. Acts too young for age d		E	0 1 2 3	41. Physically attacks people
I	0 1 2 3	a 2. Makes odd noises d			0 1 2 3	42. Picks nose, skin, or other parts of body (specify):
E	0 1 2 3	b 3. Argues d				
	0 1 2 3	4. Behaves like opposite sex			0 1 2 3	a 43. Falls asleep d
E	0 1 2 3	a 5. Defiant or talks back to staff		I	0 1 2 3	a 44. Apathetic, unmotivated, or won't try d
E	0 1 2 3	6. Bragging, boasting			0 1 2 3	45. Refuses to talk
I	0 1 2 3	b 7. Doesn't concentrate or doesn't pay attention d for long		E	0 1 2 3	a 46. Disrupts group activities d
I,E	0 1 2 3	b 8. Can't get mind of certain thoughts; obsessions d (specify):			0 1 2 3	b 47. Screams d
					0 1 2 3	b 48. Secretive, keeps things to self, including refusal d to show things to teacher
	0 1 2 3	9. Doesn't sit still, restless, or hyperactive d			0 1 2 3	49. Sees things that aren't there (specify):
E	0 1 2 3	10. Clings to adults or too dependent				
I	0 1 2 3	11. Confused or seems to be in a fog		I	0 1 2 3	50. Self-conscious or easily embarrassed
	0 1 2 3	b12. Cries d			0 1 2 3	b 51. Sexual activity (specify): c
	0 1 2 3	a13. Fidgets, including with objects d				
E	0 1 2 3	b14. Cruelty, bullying, or meanness				
I	0 1 2 3	b15. Daydreams or gets lost in thoughts d		E	0 1 2 3	b 52. Shows off or clowns d
	0 1 2 3	b16. Deliberately harms self d		I	0 1 2 3	b 53. Shy or timid behavior d
E	0 1 2 3	b17. Tries to get attention of staff d		E	0 1 2 3	a 54. Explosive & unpredictable behavior d (score temper on #71)
	0 1 2 3	b18. Destroys own things d		E	0 1 2 3	a 55. Demands must be met immediately, easily frustrated
	0 1 2 3	19. Destroys property belonging to others			0 1 2 3	a 56. Easily distracted d
E	0 1 2 3	b20. Disobedient d		I	0 1 2 3	57. Stares blankly
E	0 1 2 3	a21. Disturbs other children d			0 1 2 3	a 58. Acts like feelings are hurt when criticized d
E	0 1 2 3	b22. Doesn't seem to feel guilty after misbehaving			0 1 2 3	b 59. Steals
	0 1 2 3	b23. Shows jealousy d			0 1 2 3	b 60. Stores up things he/she doesn't need, except d hobby items such as marbles (specify):
	0 1 2 3	b24. Eats, drinks, chews, or mouths things that are d not food, excluding tobacco and junk foods (specify):				
	0 1 2 3	b25. Shows fear of specific situations or stimuli d (specify):		I	0 1 2 3	61. Strange behavior (specify):
	0 1 2 3	b26. Says no one likes him/her d			0 1 2 3	62. Strange ideas (specify):
	0 1 2 3	b27. Says others are out to get him/her d				
I,E	0 1 2 3	b28. Expresses feelings of worthlessness or inferiority d		I,E	0 1 2 3	63. Stubborn, sullen, or irritable
	0 1 2 3	b29. Gets hurt, accident prone d			0 1 2 3	64. Sudden changes in mood or feelings
	0 1 2 3	b30. Gets in physical fights d			0 1 2 3	b 65. Sulks d
I,E	0 1 2 3	b31. Gets teased d			0 1 2 3	66. Suspicious
	0 1 2 3	32. Hears things that aren't there (specify):		E	0 1 2 3	67. Swearing or obscene language
					0 1 2 3	68. Talks about killing self
I	0 1 2 3	b33. Impulsive or acts without thinking, including d calling out in class			0 1 2 3	69. Talks too much
	0 1 2 3	a34. Physically isolates self from others c		E	0 1 2 3	b 70. Teases d
E	0 1 2 3	35. Lying or cheating			0 1 2 3	71. Temper tantrums or hot temper
	0 1 2 3	36. Bites fingernails			0 1 2 3	b 72. Verbal expressions of preoccupation with sex d
I	0 1 2 3	37. Nervous, highstrung, or tense		E	0 1 2 3	b 73. Threatens people
I	0 1 2 3	38. Nervous movements or twitching (specify):			0 1 2 3	74. Too concerned with neatness or cleanliness
				I	0 1 2 3	b 75. Underactive, slow moving, lacks energy, or yawns d
	0 1 2 3	a39. Overconforms to rules		I	0 1 2 3	76. Unhappy, sad, or depressed
I	0 1 2 3	40. Too fearful or anxious		E	0 1 2 3	77. Unusually loud

Total ____ Internalizing ____ Externalizing ____   Total ____ Internalizing ____ Externalizing ____

PAGE 2

Figure 7-1. Items 1-77 of the Direct Observation Form. Superscripts to the *left* of items: *a* indicates that the item has no direct counterpart on the *CBCL*, while *b* indicates that it differs slightly from the *CBCL*. Superscripts to the *right* of items: *c* indicates that the item has no direct counterpart on the *TRF*, while *d* indicates that it differs slightly from the *TRF*.

				CBCL/4-16	TRF						CBCL/4-16	TRF

CBCL/4-16   TRF

        0   1   2   3 ᵃ 78. Overly anxious to please
E   0   1   2   3 ᵇ 79. Whining tone of voice ᵈ
I   0   1   2   3   80. Withdrawn, doesn't get involved with others
        0   1   2   3   81. Worrying
        0   1   2   3 ᵇ 82. Sucks thumb, hand, or arm ᶜ
I   0   1   2   3 ᵃ 83. Fails to express self clearly, ᶜ
                              including speech defects
E   0   1   2   3 ᵃ 84. Impatient ᶜ
I,E 0   1   2   3 ᵃ 85. Tattles ᶜ
        0   1   2   3 ᵇ 86. Compulsions, repeats behavior over & over ᵈ
                              (specify): _____
        0   1   2   3 ᵃ 87. Easily led by peers ᶜ
        0   1   2   3 ᵇ 88. Clumsy, poor motor control ᵈ
I,E 0   1   2   3 ᵇ 89. Doesn't get along with peers ᵈ

Total _____ Internalizing _____ Externalizing _____

CBCL/4-16   TRF

        0   1   2   3 ᵃ 90. Runs out of class (or similar setting) ᶜ
I   0   1   2   3 ᵃ 91. Behaves irresponsibly (specify): _____
                              _____
E   0   1   2   3 ᵃ 92. Bossy ᶜ
        0   1   2   3 ᵇ 93. Plays with younger children ᵈ
E   0   1   2   3 ᵃ 94. Complains ᶜ
I   0   1   2   3 ᵃ 95. Afraid to make mistakes ᵈ
        0   1   2   3 ᵃ 96. Acts like poor loser ᶜ
                              97. Other problems (specify):
        0   1   2   3   _____
        0   1   2   3   _____
        0   1   2   3   _____

Total _____ Internalizing _____ Externalizing _____
Sum: Total Problem Score _____ Int _____ Ext _____

Boxes 1-10 represent 10-5 sec. intervals beginning at the end of each min. of observation. If child is **not on task during the 5-sec. interval, check the left box; if s/he is on task, check the right box.** Sum on-task checks to obtain on-task score ranging from 0-10. Use space below for narrative description.

1	NOT OT	ON TASK	_____
2	NOT OT	ON TASK	_____
3	NOT OT	ON TASK	_____
4	NOT OT	ON TASK	_____
5	NOT OT	ON TASK	_____
6	NOT OT	ON TASK	_____
7	NOT OT	ON TASK	_____
8	NOT OT	ON TASK	_____
9	NOT OT	ON TASK	_____
10	NOT OT	ON TASK	_____
SUM ON TASK ___			_____

PAGE 3

Figure 7-1 (cont.). Items 78-97 of the Direct Observation Form. Superscripts to the *left* of items: *a* indicates that the item has no direct counterpart on the *CBCL*, while *b* indicates that it differs slightly from the *CBCL*. Superscripts to the *right* of items: *c* indicates that the item has no direct counterpart on the *TRF*, while *d* indicates that it differs slightly from the *TRF*.

items, and discussing disagreements with another observer who rates the same sessions. It is important to follow the scoring rules listed on the DOF and to avoid scoring more than one item for a particular behavior. Detailed rules for scoring specific items are printed on the Revised Edition of the DOF completed in 1986.

SCORES AND SCALES OF THE DOF

The scores on the DOF are to be averaged over several observational sessions to obtain a stable index of behavior. Comparisons with one or two "control" children are also recommended to provide a standard of comparison within the target child's own classroom. Table 7-1 shows the scales of the DOF and lists the narrow-band syndromes derived from factor analyses of DOFs completed on 212 clinically-referred 5-14-year-old children and normed on 287 children who were ob-

Table 7-1
Scales Scored from the Direct Observation Form[a]

On-Task
Total Problems
Internalizing
Externalizing

Narrow-Band Syndromes

Withdrawn-Inattentive
Nervous-Obsessive
Depressed
Hyperactive
Attention Demanding
Aggressive

[a]Scales were derived from ratings of classroom observations of 212 clinically-referred children and normed on 287 nonreferred children.

served in regular classrooms of 45 schools in 23 public and parochial school systems located in Vermont, Nebraska, and Oregon. The DOF is scored for boys and girls on the same profile. Hand- and computer-scored versions of the DOF profile are available for on-task, total problem, Internalizing, and Externalizing scores. The narrow-band scales are included only on the computer-scored profile because the computation of narrow-band scales is too complex to be done by hand.

On-Task, Internalizing, Externalizing, and Total Problem Scales

Figure 7-2 shows the computer-scored version of the on-task and broad-band scales for 11-year-old Michael, the boy discussed in Chapters 3, 5, and 6. Table 7-2 explains each score of the profile.

The DOF scores shown in Figure 7-2 were obtained by averaging Michael's scores and those of two control boys observed in school on three occasions. There are no clinical cutoffs for the on-task scores. However, the mean on-task scores can easily be converted to percentages, showing that Michael was on-task an average of 65% of the time, compared to 90% for the control boys. Michael's total problem score of 8.5 was in the clinical range (T score = 70; >93rd percentile), while the mean total problem score of 4.0 for the control boys was in the normal range. Michael's Internalizing score of 1.0 was in the normal range, while his Externalizing score of 1.5 was in the clinical range (>94th percentile).

Narrow-Band Scales

Only raw scores and percentile cutoffs are provided for the narrow-band scales of the DOF, because low variability in scores precluded computing T scores. Figure 7-3 shows the computer-scored version of the DOF narrow-band scales for 11-year-old Michael, while Table 7-3 explains each score on the profile.

DIRECT OBSERVATION FORM

DIRECT OBSERVATION FORM OF THE CHILD BEHAVIOR CHECKLIST

```
OTHER PROBLEMS *        MEAN ON-TASK
  I     C                  SCORE              INTERNALIZING  EXTERNALIZING    TOTAL PROBLEM SCORE
0.0   0.0  4.OPP SEX      _____                                                          _____  T SCORE
0.0   0.0 12.CRIES       -I   10.0   I-      -I  22.5+  I  22.5+  I-         -I  61.0+  I-100
0.0   0.0 16.HARMS       -I          I-      -I  22.0   I  22.0   I-         -I         I-      CASE#
            SELF         -I   (C)    I-      -I         I         I-         -I         I-          MICHAEL
0.0   0.0 18.DS OWN      -I          I-      -I  21.0   I  21.0   I-         -I  43.0  I-95
0.0   0.0 19.DS OTH      -I    8.0   I-      -I         I         I-         -I         I-      SEX: BOY
0.0   0.0 23.JEALOS      -I          I-      -I  20.0   I  20.0   I-         -I         I-
0.0   0.0 24.NNFOOD      -I    7.0   I-      -I         I         I-         -I  23.0  I-90  AGE: 11
0.0   0.0 25.FEARS       -I   (I)    I-      -I  19.0   I  19.0   I-         -I         I-
0.0   0.0 26.UNLIKD      -I    6.0   I-      -I         I         I-         -I         I-      OBSERVER: 4
0.0   0.0 27.PERSEC      -I          I-      -I  18.0   I  18.0   I-         -I  18.0  I-85
0.0   0.0 29.ACCDNT      -I    5.0   I-      -I         I         I-         -I         I-      SETTING: 1
            PRONE        -I          I-      -I  17.0   I  17.0   I-         -I         I-
0.0   0.0 30.FIGHTS      -I    4.0   I-      -I         I         I-         -I  15.0  I-80  NUMBER OF
0.0   0.0 32.HEARS       -I          I-      -I  16.0   I  16.0   I-         -I         I-      OBSERVATIONS:
            THINGS            3.0   I-      -I         I         I-         -I         I-        I: 3
0.0   0.0 34.ISOLAT      -I          I-      -I  15.0   I  15.0   I-         -I  11.5  I-75      C1: 3
0.0   0.0 39.CONFRM      -I    2.0   I-      -I         I         I-         -I         I-        C2: 3
0.0   0.0 42.PICKS       -I          I-      -I  14.0   I  14.0   I-         -I         I-
0.0   0.0 43.SLEEPS      -I    1.0   I-      -I         I         I-         -I   (I)  I-70  OBSRV DATES
0.0   0.0 45.NO TLK      -I          I-      -I  13.0   I  13.0   I-         -I         I-      FOR I CHILD:
0.0   0.0 47.SCREAM      -I    0.0   I-      -I         I         I-      %ILE-I         I-      1. 05/15/87
0.0   0.0 48.SECRET      -I_____  I-      -I  12.0   I  12.0   I-      93-I----6.0---I-65  2. 05/15/87
0.0   0.0 49.SEES        -I          I-      -I         I         I-         -I         I-      3. 05/15/87
            THINGS          ON-TASK          -I  11.0   I  11.0   I-         -I         I-      4. NONE
0.0   0.0 51.SEXPRB        MEAN SCORES       -I         I         I-         -I       I-60      5. NONE
0.0   0.0 58.HURT            I     C         -I  10.0   I  10.0   I-         -I   5.0  I-      6. NONE
            FEELING        6.5   9.0         -I         I         I-       75-I         I-
0.0   0.0 59.STEALS                          -I   9.0   I   9.0   I-         -I       I-55
0.0   0.0 60.HOARDS                          -I         I         I-         -I  (C)  I-
0.0   0.0 62.STRANG                          -I   8.0   I   8.0   I-         -I         I-
            IDEAS                            -I         I         I-         -I       I-50
0.0   0.0 64.MOODY                           -I   7.0   I   7.0   I-         -I   3.0  I-
0.0   0.0 65.SULKS                           -I         I         I-         -I         I-
0.0   0.0 66.SUSPCS                          -I   6.0   I   6.0   I-         -I       I-45
0.0   0.0 68.TALKS       * PROBLEMS NOT SCORED -I       I         I-       25-I   2.0  I-
            SUICID         ON NARROW BAND     -I   5.0   I   5.0   I-         -I         I-
0.0   0.0 71.TEMPER       SCALES ON PAGE 1    -I        I         I-         -I       I-40
0.0   0.0 72.SEX                             -I   4.0   I   4.0   I-         -I   1.0  I-
            PREOCC                           -I         I         I-         -I         I-
0.0   0.0 74.NEAT                            -I   3.0   I   3.0   I-         -I       I-35
0.0   0.0 78.ANX TO                          -I         I         I-         -I         I-
            PLEASE         COPYRIGHT 1987   94%ILE-I-----2.0-----I   2.0   I-       3-I   0.0  I-
0.0   0.0 81.WORRY        T. ACHENBACH, PH.D. -I        I   (I)   I-
0.0   0.0 82.THUMB        DEPT OF PSYCHIATRY  -I  (I)   I-----1.0-----I-94%ILE
0.0   0.0 86.COMPUL       UNIVERSITY OF VERMONT -I      I         I-      TOTAL PROBLEM
0.0   0.0 87.LED          BURLINGTON, VT 05401 -I (C)__I__  (C)__I-      MEAN SCORE
0.0   0.0 88.CLUMSY                                                         I     C
0.0   0.0 90.RN OUT                          INTERNALIZING   EXTERNALIZING  8.5   4.0
0.0   0.0 93.PREFER                          MEAN SCORES    MEAN SCORES     T SCORE
            YNG CH                             I     C        I     C         I     C
0.0   0.0 96.POOR                            1.0   0.0      1.5   0.0       70    54
            LOSER
0.0   0.0 97.OTHER
```

Figure 7-2. Computer-scored version of the DOF on-task and broad-band scale scores for 11-year-old Michael (designated "I") and the averaged scores for two control boys (designated "C"). Note that the clinical cutoff is the 93rd percentile for the total problem score and the 94th percentile for Internalizing and Externalizing scores. There is no cutoff for the on-task score.

Table 7-2
Explanations of Scores on the On-Task and Broad-Band Problem Scales of the DOF Profile

I, C: the letter "I" indicates the mean score for the Identified child, while the letter "C" indicates the mean score for the Control children.

Percentiles: the percent of children in the normative sample of nonreferred children who obtained a score less than or equal to each raw score. A range of percentiles is listed for the total problem scores, while only percentiles marking the clinical cutoffs are shown for Internalizing and Externalizing.

T scores: standard scores based on the percentiles of the raw scores for the normative sample of nonreferred children. T scores are given only for the total problem score, but not for Internalizing, Externalizing, or on-task scores.

Normal range: scores at or below the cutoff dividing the normative sample of nonreferred children from the clinically-referred children. Scores above the 93rd percentile on the total problem score and above the 94th percentile on Internalizing and Externalizing scales are considered to be in the clinical range. There is no clinical cutoff for on-task scores.

On-task mean score: the mean raw score for the number of intervals in which the child was judged to be on-task during each of the 10 one-minute observation periods, rounded to the nearest .5.

Internalizing mean score: mean raw score for the sum of the 0s, 1s, 2s, and 3s for the Internalizing items, rounded to the nearest .5.

Externalizing mean score: mean raw score for the sum of the 0s, 1s, 2s, and 3s for the Externalizing items, rounded to the nearest .5.

Total problem mean score: mean raw score for the sum of the 0s, 1s, 2s, and 3s for the 97 problem items, rounded to the nearest .5.

Total T score: normalized T score for the total problem score based on the raw scores for the normative sample of nonreferred children.

Other problems: mean raw scores of 0s, 1s, 2s, and 3s for items counted in the total problem score, but not included in scores for any of the narrow-band scales.

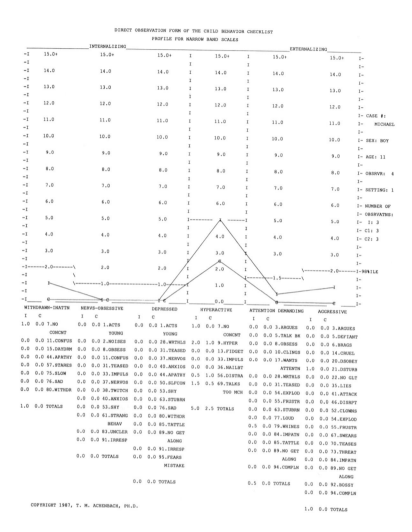

Figure 7-3. Computer-scored version of the DOF narrow-band scale scores for 11-year-old Michael (designated "I") and the averaged scores for two control boys (designated "C"). Note that the broken line for the clinical cutoff at the 98th percentile varies because they are based directly on raw scores (T scores are not computed for the DOF narrow-band scales).

Table 7-3
Explanations of Scores on the Narrow-Band Scales
of the DOF Profile

I, C: the letter "I" indicates the mean score of the Identified child, while the letter "C" indicates the mean score of the Control children.

Normal range: scores at or below the broken line that marks the 98th percentile of the normative sample. Scores above the broken line are considered to be in the clinical range. The location of the broken line showing the cutoff varies from one scale to another, because of variation in raw scores corresponding to the 98th percentile.

Narrow-band total score: the mean raw score obtained by summing the 0s, 1s, 2s, and 3s entered for each item on the scale, rounded to the nearest .5.

Figure 7-3 shows the pattern of Michael's scores on the narrow-band scales of the DOF (solid line) compared with those of the control boys (broken line). Michael's scores were in the normal range on all but one of the six scales. His score of 5.0 on the Hyperactive scale was at the clinical cutoff (98th percentile), with scores on items *7. Doesn't concentrate or doesn't pay attention for long*; *9. Doesn't sit still, restless, or hyperactive*; *56. Easily distracted*; and *69. Talks too much*. The scores of the control boys were in the normal range on all scales.

Summary of Cutoffs and Mean Scores

Table 7-4 summarizes the cutoffs between the normal and clinical range for the scales of the DOF. Cutoffs are listed in terms of raw scores and percentiles for each scale except the on-task score, which has no cutoff. Table 7-4 also lists the mean scores and standard deviations for classroom observations of children referred for outpatient mental health or special school services and control children observed in the same classrooms.

Table 7-4
Summary of Cutoffs and Mean Scores for DOF Scales

Scale	Cutoffs[a]		Mean Scores[b]	
	Raw Score	%ile	Clinical	Control
On-Task	No Clinical Cutoffs		6.6 (2.1)	8.9 (1.0)
Total Problems	6.0	93	9.1 (4.1)	3.5 (1.9)
Internalizing	2.0	94	2.4 (1.9)	.6 (.8)
Externalizing	1.0	94	1.6 (1.8)	.2 (.6)
Withdrawn–Inattentive	2.0	98	1.7 (1.7)	.5 (.8)
Nervous-Obsessive	1.0	98	.8 (.8)	.1 (.3)
Depressed	1.0	98	.6 (1.1)	.1 (.4)
Hyperactive	5.0	98	5.0 (2.8)	2.5 (1.6)
Attention Demanding	1.5	98	.7 (1.1)	.1 (.4)
Aggressive	2.0	98	1.2 (1.3)	.2 (.5)

[a]Scores *above* the cutoffs are in the clinical range
[b]Standard deviations are in parentheses. The clinical group comprised 137 elementary school children referred for outpatient mental health or special school services who were observed in 43 schools of 21 Vermont public and parochial school systems. The control group consisted of 274 children observed as controls in the same classrooms as the referred children. The means and standard deviations were obtained by averaging the mean of all boys' scores with the mean of all girls' scores, thus weighting both sexes equally.

SUMMARY

The DOF is designed for recording behavior problems and on-task behavior observed over 10-minute intervals in group settings such as school classrooms and recess. The DOF differs from the other forms of the CBCL in being scored for a specific time sample of behavior and having 4-step rating scales. The DOF scoring profile is designed to compare the target child with one or two "control" children observed in the same setting. To obtain a stable index of behavior, the DOF scores for each child are to be averaged over three to six observational sessions.

The scales for scoring the DOF are based on data for 5- to 14-year-old children. On-Task, Total Problems, Internalizing, and Externalizing are scorable by hand or computer, but the narrow-band scales listed in Table 7-1 are scorable only by computer, because the averaging of scores across occasions and across control subjects is too complex to do by hand. Table 7-4 summarizes mean scale scores, as well as cutoffs that distinguish between the normal and clinical ranges.

Chapter 8
Reporting Results of Multiaxial
Empirically-Based Assessment

The written report is an important component of the assessment process, often serving as the main vehicle for integrating findings, formulating conclusions, and communicating recommendations. In this chapter, we present examples of reports illustrating how the results of our empirically-based measures can be combined with information from other sources. Other formats have been presented elsewhere (e.g., Applebaum, 1970; Fischer, 1973, 1979; Kaufman, 1979; Knoff, 1986; Sattler, 1987), and readers should choose formats compatible with their personal style. Formats and degree of detail also depend on the nature of referral questions and needs of intended recipients.

Reports to parents who have requested the evaluation and to professionals closely involved in a case would typically be the most comprehensive. This type of report usually includes detailed background information, test results, current functioning, and dynamics of the case, followed by specific recommendations. Other comprehensive reports, such as those for forensic evaluations (Chapter 9), might require different formats, such as a focus on specific questions from the court. Unlike these comprehensive evaluations, reports written for institutional use, such as notes for a medical record, and communications with people needing less detail, such as pediatricians, case workers, and teachers, would usually be much shorter, presenting only summaries of the findings and recommendations.

We provide three examples of reports on the findings for 11-year-old Michael, whose CBCL/4-16, TRF, YSR, and DOF profiles were presented in previous chapters. The first example illustrates a comprehensive report intended for communicating to the main referral agents and professionals closely involved in the case. The second example illustrates how the same findings can be summarized for a medical record or communications with the family pediatrician. The third example illustrates a summary report emphasizing recommendations for school staff.

EXAMPLE 1: A COMPREHENSIVE EVALUATION REPORT

The comprehensive evaluation report presents and interprets data obtained from all sources in the multiaxial model. It should include relevant aspects of the child's history, results of all assessment procedures, a case formulation, and recommendations, as described below.

After stating the child's name, birthdate, age, grade, and date of examination, the report begins with the *Reason for Referral*, which summarizes the questions prompting the evaluation. The *Assessment Procedures* section lists specific procedures in the order in which they are discussed in the report, followed by general procedures, such as interviews and record reviews. A section on *Background Information* presents details of the child's development, educational history, relevant medical factors, and information obtained from interviews of informants, such as parents, teachers, and other practitioners. The results of previous evaluations should also be summarized.

A brief description of observations and impressions of the child is provided in a section titled *Behavior During Evaluation*. Observations particularly relevant to the referral questions should be noted, as well as observations that can lead to specific recommendations. A statement about the likely validity of test results is also desirable. The *Results* section reports scores and their interpretations. Our example presents findings separately for each instrument and then summarizes findings from other clinical procedures, including personality tests and the interview with Michael. We took this approach to highlight how findings can be reported from the CBCL/4-16, TRF, YSR, and DOF. An alternative approach would be to group the findings into broader categories, such as results from ability and achievement tests, ratings by different informants, and results from interviews and personality tests.

The *Formulation* synthesizes and integrates findings from all sources, describing the child's current functioning in different environments and the dynamics of interactions with family, school staff, and other important people. The formulation should include hypotheses about causal factors involved in the child's problems, the feasibility of particular interventions, and realistic goals. Based on the formulation, *Recommendations* are outlined for appropriate interventions, addressing the initial referral questions and any new concerns that emerged in the course of evaluation. The recommendations should pinpoint targets for change and methods for helping the child and family. To be effective, recommendations need to be concrete, practical, and tailored to the specific needs of the child and family. The following is an example of a comprehensive evaluation report on 11-year-old Michael.

EVALUATION REPORT

Name: Michael Jones
Date of birth: 11/10/75
Age: 11 years, 6 months
Grade: Fourth
Date of examination: 5/15/87

Reason for Referral

Michael was brought for an evaluation by his mother at the suggestion of the special education director of his school. He was having learning and behavioral problems at school, and was becoming increasingly difficult to control at home. In spite of remedial reading services at school, his grades were poor and he was often in trouble. The evaluation was requested to assess Michael's cognitive, behavioral, and emotional functioning in order to obtain recommendations for his educational program and behavior management at home and at school.

Assessment Procedures

Wechsler Intelligence Scale for Children-Revised (WISC-R)
Individual achievement tests
Child Behavior Checklist (CBCL/4-16)
Teacher's Report Form (TRF)
Youth Self-Report Form (YSR)
Direct Observation Form (DOF)
Social and personality tests
Clinical interview with Michael
Interviews with mother and teacher
Review of educational and medical records

Background Information

Michael was the youngest of two children. His parents were recently separated following several years of marital conflict. Michael lived with his mother and sister (age 15) at the time of the evaluation. The father was employed as a truck driver and the mother as a secretary. Michael's mother reported that the father had a history of alcohol abuse and was physically abusive toward her on several occasions prior to their separation. She reported that Michael's behavior at home had been a problem since he was young, but that he had recently become more defiant and aggressive and had begun lying and stealing. She said Michael had always been very active and prone to temper tantrums. His early physical development was normal, with no major illnesses or physical problems, except for chronic ear infections. He was slightly delayed in speech development and had difficulty learning since he entered school. He was diagnosed by a child psychiatrist as having Attention Deficit Disorder with Hyperactivity at age 9. The psychiatrist prescribed stimulant medication and then tricyclic antidepressants, but Mrs. Jones reported little benefit. Although teachers reported some improvement in attention span, the medication was discontinued after one year.

At the time of the present evaluation, Michael was in fourth grade, having previously repeated Kindergarten and third grade. Michael's teacher described him as very restless, with a short attention span. She said he demanded constant attention, was often out of his seat, and was often punished for incomplete assignments and fighting on the playground. His behavior was much more appropriate in one-to-one or small group situations. He had received remedial reading services since first grade, and had just been referred for evaluation for special education. Group ability and achievement tests at school showed overall ability in the average range and low average achievement in vocabulary and reading comprehension (Metropolitan Achievement Test, 10th and 9th percentiles, respectively). His achievement in mathematics was in the average range (Metropolitan Achievement Test, 14th to 28th percentiles).

Behavior During Evaluation

Michael was very friendly and cooperative throughout the testing and interview session. He was not unusually restless and showed generally good attention. His approach to tasks was impulsive, however, and he was easily discouraged on difficult items. Nevertheless, he responded well to praise and encouragement to slow down and be more careful. He was open and honest about personal and family matters, freely offering many comments. Difficulties in the home and the recent separation of his parents were major concerns. Overall, the results appear to be a valid sample of his current functioning.

Results

On the *Wechsler Intelligence Test for Children-Revised* (WISC-R), Michael scored in the average range for verbal ability (VIQ = 96), in the very superior range for performance ability (PIQ = 139), and in the high average range for overall ability (FSIQ = 118). According to Sattler (1987), the chances are 95 out of 100 that Michael's true full scale IQ lies between 112 and 124. The 43-point discrepancy between his verbal and performance IQ scores is highly significant, suggesting much greater strength in nonverbal than verbal areas. Subtest scatter revealed significant strengths in spatial reasoning, but relative weakness in acquired knowledge. Scores for conceptual reasoning and freedom from distractibility were in the average range.

On the *verbal* subtests of the WISC-R, Michael obtained low average to average scores in all areas including general information, abstract verbal reasoning, numerical reasoning and concentration, expressive vocabulary, practical reasoning, and short-term auditory attention span. On the *performance* subtests, Michael showed above average scores in visual discrimination of fine detail, visual sequencing around social themes, abstract nonverbal reasoning, recognition of part-whole relations in familiar objects, and visual-motor speed. His visual-motor planning was in the average range. The following breakdown gives Michael's scores on the subtests of the WISC-R. A score of 7 to 13 generally indicates the average range.

Verbal		*Performance*	
Information	8	Picture Completion	16
Similarities	8	Picture Arrangement	16
Arithmetic	9	Block Design	14
Vocabulary	10	Object Assembly	17
Comprehension	12	Coding	15
Digit Span	7	Mazes	11

The *Peabody Individual Achievement Test* (PIAT) was administered to assess Michael's achievement and approach to educational tasks. Compared to norms for his age, Michael scored below average in reading recognition and spelling, low average in reading comprehension, and average in mathematics and general information. Compared to norms for his grade, Michael's scores ranged from high average in mathematics to low average in reading recognition and spelling. The grade level equivalents showed that he was still not achieving up to his present grade in reading and spelling, despite having repeated two grades. The following breakdown gives Michael's scores on the subtests of the PIAT in grade level equivalents (GLE), percentiles, and standard scores (SS) compared to norms for his grade and age. Standard scores have a mean of 100 and standard deviation of 15. Asterisks indicate scores more than 1.5 standard deviations below his WISC-R full-scale IQ.

PIAT Subtest	GLE	Grade %ile	Grade SS	Age %ile	Age SS
Mathematics	7.4	82	114	51	100
Reading Recognition	3.3	18	86*	8	79*
Reading Comprehension	4.2	37	95*	17	86*
Spelling	3.5	19	87*	6	77*
General Information	5.1	55	102	28	91*

The *Test of Written Language* (TOWL) and *Test of Written Spelling* (TWS) further documented deficits in written language (Written Language Quotient = 75; Written Spelling Quotient = 77), while the *Test of Reading Comprehension* (TORC) showed exceptionally poor reading skills (Reading Comprehension Quotient = 65).

The *Child Behavior Checklist* (CBCL/4-16) was completed by Michael's mother to assess his social competence and behavioral/emotional problems. The CBCL/4-16 yielded a total competence score in the clinical range (below 10th percentile) compared to norms for boys aged 6-11. While Michael's score on the Activities scale was in the normal range, his scores on the Social and School scales were in the clinical range (below 2nd percentile). His mother reported participation in several individual sports and some chores at home, but he belonged to no social organizations, had only one close friend, had difficulty getting along with other children in school, and was receiving special school services. Michael's Internalizing, Externalizing, and total problem scores were all in the clinical range (above 90th percentile) for boys aged 6-11. He also scored in the clinical range on the Depressed, Uncommunicative, Obsessive-Compulsive, Social Withdrawal, Hyperactive, Aggressive, and Delinquent scales (above 98th percentile), but in the normal range on the Schizoid-Anxious and Somatic Complaints scales. Michael's overall pattern of problems was most similar to that of the Hyperactive and Delinquent profile types, indicating greatest deviance in hyperactivity and rule-breaking behavior. It should be noted, however, that Michael had *not* come to the attention of the police or juvenile justice system.

The *Teacher's Report Form* (TRF) was completed by Michael's fourth grade teacher to assess his adaptive functioning and behavioral/emotional problems in school. The TRF yielded a total score for adaptive functioning in the clinical range (below 13th percentile) compared to norms for boys aged 6-11. Compared to typical pupils, Michael's teacher rated him as working much less hard, behaving much less appropriately, learning somewhat less, and slightly less happy. She rated his school performance as far below grade level in spelling and writing, somewhat below grade in reading, at grade level in science and social studies, and above grade level in math. Michael's Externalizing and total problem scores were in the clinical range (above 89th percentile) compared to norms for boys aged 6-11, but his Internalizing score was in the normal range. Michael's score on the Aggressive scale was in the clinical range (above 98th percentile), while scores on all other scales were in the normal range. The Aggressive scale included scores for arguing, defiance, disobedience, impulsiveness, and various problems in peer relations, but no lying or stealing as had been reported by his mother. Though his teacher scored Michael on many items of the Inattentive and Nervous-Overactive scales, his total scores on both these scales were in the normal range. The teacher also indicated destructiveness toward property but no self-destructive behavior.

The *Youth Self-Report* (YSR) was completed by Michael to provide his own views of his competence and behavior. Since Michael's reading skills were poor, the psychologist read the YSR to him during their evaluation session. Michael's self-ratings on the Activities and Social scales were in the normal range, although his score on the Social scale was close to the clinical cutoff. He reported interests in baseball and football, but no involvement in social organizations. He reported having one friend whom he saw once or twice a week. He rated his school performance below average in all areas, except math, which he rated as above average. Michael's total problem score on the YSR was in the normal range for boys aged 11-18 (below 89th percentile). His scores on the Internalizing and Externalizing scales and all the narrow-band scales were also in the normal range, including the Aggressive scale, which was in sharp contrast to parent and teacher ratings. He did, however, acknowledge some problems with unpopularity and fears, occasional lying, and disobedience at home and school.

The *Direct Observation Form* (DOF) was used by the school guidance counselor to rate Michael's behavior on three occasions in the classroom and twice at recess. In the classroom, Michael was on-task an average of only 65% of the time compared to 90% for two boys selected for comparison in the same class. His total problem score was in the clinical range (above 93rd percentile), as was his Externalizing score (above 94th percentile), compared to norms for boys and girls aged 5-14. His Internalizing score was in the normal range, as were all scores for the two comparison boys. Michael's score on the DOF Hyperactive scale was at the clinical cutoff (98th percentile), including scores for difficulty concentrating, restlessness, being easily distracted, and talking too much. Scores on all other DOF scales were in the normal range. At recess, the observer noted that Michael argued constantly about the rules of games and teased and bossed other children. No physical fights with other children were observed.

On various *social reasoning tasks and personality measures*, Michael exhibited a low average self-concept, an external locus of control, and a generally aggressive approach to solving social problems and conflict. He showed a clear sense of right and wrong and preconventional style of moral reasoning, focusing on rewards and punishments as consequences of behavior. In the *clinical interview*, Michael complained of being picked on by peers in both verbal and physical ways. He had only vague notions of what precipitated his social problems, frequently blaming problems on others. Family issues were a major concern. He felt rejected by his parents and resented their frequent use of corporal punishment. Nonetheless, Michael expressed affection for both parents and wished they would reunite. Michael was negative about most aspects of school, especially reading and writing. He said he enjoyed small group instruction in his remedial reading class. He felt his best skills were in math and expressed interests in prevocational and science classes with projects. He was also very positive about a behavioral contract he had recently negotiated with his teacher and guidance counselor at school.

Formulation

Michael was brought for a psychological evaluation by his mother to assess learning and behavioral/emotional problems. The results of the evaluation showed high average intelligence, with average verbal ability but very superior nonverbal ability. The very large discrepancy between Michael's verbal and nonverbal ability indicated a significant unevenness in cognitive functioning. He displayed marked strengths in visual-spatial and mechanical areas, in contrast to relative weaknesses in attention and abstract verbal reasoning.

Achievement testing showed significant deficits in reading and writing, reflecting Michael's long standing school learning problems. The large discrepancy between Michael's ability and achievement test scores in reading and written language (more than 2 standard deviations) qualify him for special education as a learning disabled child. His math achievement, on the other hand, was in the average range, indicating that learning disabilities do not affect all areas of school performance. Unfortunately, much of the standard elementary school curriculum focuses on areas where Michael is weakest by placing a premium on verbal skills and good attention, while his superior visual-spatial skills will not be tapped until later, when he can take vocational courses. Special education services are, therefore, vital to enable Michael to achieve up to his potential. His poor achievement in reading and writing, despite repeating two grades, testifies to his need for more intensive educational interventions.

A variety of behavioral and personality measures indicated poor social competence and behavioral/emotional problems accompanying Michael's learning disabilities. Both his mother and teacher reported behavior problems beyond normal levels for boys his age. The pattern of problems was primarily of an externalizing, aggressive nature, warranting a DSM-III-R diagnosis of Oppositional Defiant Disorder. Michael is often defiant and noncompliant at home, occasionally lies and steals, and is argumentative and disruptive at school. Michael's mother reported problems related to depression and difficulty communicating as well, consistent with his weak verbal skills. However, these problems seemed less severe in the more structured school environment. There was also evidence of overactivity and inattention consistent with a previous psychiatric diagnosis of Attention Deficit Disorder with Hyperactivity, but, again, these problems were more prevalent at home than at school and not as severe as Michael's other conduct problems.

Michael's learning disabilities could easily account for some of his behavioral/emotional problems due to poor attention, low frustration tolerance, and the negative impact of school failure on his self-esteem. At the same time, family conflict is a significant additional factor influencing Michael's behavior. The instability of the home situation and recent separation of his parents have produced considerable stress in Michael, which he acts out in external ways. He is highly reactive to conflict at home, but has limited understanding of his own emotional reactions. This leads to power struggles and agitated, hyperactive, and aggressive behavior. The power struggles often extend beyond the family, producing negative interactions with authority figures and peers at school. Being external in locus of control, Michael has difficulty recognizing his own part in social conflicts, often viewing himself as a victim and seldom acknowledging any connection between his behavior and its effect on others. His low scores on self-ratings of behavior problems, in contrast to high scores by other informants, demonstrate Michael's insensitivity to his deviant behavior. To be successful, a therapeutic intervention must, therefore, take account of Michael's lack of insight and the impact of his learning disabilities, as well as the larger context of family conflict.

Recommendations

Based on the present evaluation, the following recommendations are offered regarding Michael's educational program and behavioral/emotional needs.

A. Educational Program

1. Special education services for the learning disabled are recommended in the areas of reading recognition, reading comprehension, and written expression. Ideally, Michael's Individual Education Plan (IEP) should include daily services in these areas through one-to-one or small group instruction. While Michael is most eligible for special education under the learning disability category, it is important that his IEP also address behavioral/emotional needs in school.

2. No further grade retentions should be used, since Michael is already two grades behind children his age.

3. Special services in reading should be based on a multisensory approach that capitalizes on Michael's strengths in visual perception. A program organized around spelling patterns and word families would be most appropriate, utilizing visual, auditory, and kinesthetic modalities. Training in reading recognition and spelling skills should be integrated into one program if possible.

4. Instruction in reading comprehension should focus on developing both literal and inferential comprehension, organizational skills, and a better understanding of text structure and meaning. Use of visual cues could be particularly helpful, since Michael scored much higher on the PIAT reading comprehension than on the TORC, which does not use pictures. Easy reading materials (e.g., high interest-low vocabulary texts) would improve Michael's speed and fluency as well as his capacity to predict meaning in reading.

5. Michael's IEP also needs to focus on developing better writing skills. Using visual aids and outlines would help to develop organizational skills for writing. Exercises on a microcomputer could be particularly effective for focusing on spelling and grammatical structure, as well as organizing and editing drafts of written work.

6. Michael should remain in a mainstream classroom for math, science, and any prevocational courses. Classroom adaptations may be necessary, however, because of his problems in concentration and task completion.

7. Reading and writing assignments in mainstream classes may need to be adapted by reducing their length and the amount of material presented at one time. Short, frequent assignments in an orderly sequence are preferable to long-term projects. Easy reading materials may also be necessary to adapt to Michael's learning disability. Clear, concise outlines of daily assignments are important for enhancing his organizational skills.

8. A check and point system is recommended to reinforce on-task behavior and completion of assignments and to reduce aggressive, noncompliant behavior in school. This could consist of a simple recording form for each day on which the teacher checks whether Michael completed assigned work in each subject and awards points for specified behaviors, such as staying in his seat, raising his hand for assistance, and working quietly. The system should begin with modest, well-defined daily and weekly goals tied to a menu of rewards. The goals can be gradually increased as productivity improves. A similar system could be developed to reduce aggressive behavior during recess and less structured time.

9. Training in self-monitoring strategies and study skills is recommended to improve on-task behavior and work completion, along with the check and point system outlined above. Positive reinforcement for slowing down and working carefully has already proven effective with Michael. Frequent verbal repetition of expectations and consequences would also be helpful.

10. Early enrollment in a vocationally-oriented program is recommended to improve Michael's motivation and to capitalize on his cognitive strengths in visual-spatial areas.

B. Behavioral Management and Emotional Needs

1. A behavior modification program is recommended as the the main therapeutic strategy with Michael outside of school. The initial focus of such a program should be on reducing aggressive, antisocial, and noncompliant behavior. Michael and his mother should work with a child psychologist trained in behavioral techniques. Russell Barkley's parent training program is an example of a good approach for Michael. (Russell A. Barkley, *Defiant Children: A Clinician's Manual for Parent Training*, New York: Guilford Press, 1987.)

2. It is especially important that nonaggressive strategies for controlling Michael be utilized at home, since corporal punishment tends to raise his stress level and provides inappropriate examples for dealing with social problems. Time-outs, loss of privileges, and behavioral contracts are preferable to corporal punishment. Since a behavioral contract was effective at school, a similar approach could be developed at home.

3. Training in social problem solving skills is also recommended for Michael at home and at school. The program should focus on defining social problems, generating alternative solutions, evaluating consequences, and developing and modeling more socially appropriate behavior. Focusing on how to respond to name-calling would be a good starting point, since this has been a particular problem leading to confrontations with peers at school.

4. Short-term counseling for Michael may also be helpful to address emotional issues around his parents' separation and family conflict. However, Michael's relatively low verbal IQ and his failure to acknowledge his own behavior problems suggest that he is probably not a good candidate for long-term individual psychotherapy. Behavioral approaches are likely to be more effective, given his high Externalizing scores on the CBCL/4-16 and TRF, preconventional style of moral reasoning, and external locus of control on personality measures.

5. To develop better social competence, Michael needs to be more involved in social organizations and structured social activities. A local summer camp for troubled children offers good opportunities. Participation in a Big Brother program could provide a positive male role model for him. Participation in team sports, YMCA programs, and other organized activities are further examples.

6. Participation in a peer tutoring situation at school would provide an additional opportunity for Michael to develop better social relations. The best approach might be to have Michael tutor another child in an area of his strength, such as math, thereby enhancing his self-esteem and sense of social responsibility.

7. Michael's parents need to recognize that family issues and conflict have a serious impact on Michael. Stability and consistency in the home are necessary to facilitate improvements in his behavior. Marital counseling or divorce mediation could be helpful to resolve family issues. Evaluation of the father's alcohol problems might also be appropriate to obtain recommendations for possible treatment.

8. Michael's learning disabilities and significant family problems suggest that Attention Deficit-Hyperactivity Disorder is not the primary cause of his behavior and learning problems. Although Michael displays some of the characteristics of Attention Deficit-Hyperactivity Disorder, this appears less central than other concerns outlined above. It is not clear whether medication is indicated, but it is not recommended without other interventions. Once the interventions outlined above are in place, further evaluation by a physician for medication may be warranted. If medication is reinstated, Michael's behavior should be carefully monitored with regular reports from parents and teachers. One approach is to have parents and teachers complete the Conners rating scales (Goyette, Conners, & Ulrich, 1978) weekly and chart the results concurrently with changes in the dosage.

9. A follow-up assessment with the CBCL/4-16, TRF, and YSR is recommended in about one year to evaluate the effects of interventions.

Evaluator _____

cc: Mr. and Mrs. Jones
     Mr. Joseph Smith, Special Education Director

EXAMPLE 2: SUMMARY REPORT OF AN EVALUATION

Written communications to other practitioners are often most effective in the form of a brief summary report, rather than a detailed report like that in Example 1. The summary should present a clear, succinct description of relevant history leading to the referral, followed by major findings and recommendations. This type of report would be appropriate for other practitioners who have an ongoing relationship with the child and family, such as the pediatrician or a case worker, or practitioners who will be conducting further evaluations or treatment, such as a neurologist. A summary report is also often the most appropriate format for a general clinic file or medical record. In some cases, the practitioner may choose to write both a detailed, comprehensive report for the main referral agent and his/her personal file and a summary report for other recipients, noting that the comprehensive report is available if appropriate releases are obtained. This approach enables the practitioner to adapt the style and format of each report to the needs and sophistication of different recipients. Writing comprehensive and summary reports also facilitates communication with all important parties, while protecting the confidentiality of sensitive information and specific test scores.

The following example is a summary report of Michael's clinical evaluation written for the family pediatrician. The pediatrician continued to follow Michael's case and consult with the mother on behavior management issues. Because the pediatrician was particularly concerned about the earlier diagnosis of Attention Deficit Disorder with Hyperactivity, the summary of results includes discussion of DSM-III-R diagnoses for Michael and the recommendations address the question of medication along with other interventions.

SUMMARY OF EVALUATION

Re: Michael Jones
Date of birth: 11/10/75
Age: 11 years, 6 months
Grade: Fourth
Date of examination: 5/15/87

Presenting Problems and History

Michael Jones was brought for evaluation by his mother at the suggestion of the special education director in his school. He had been experiencing learning and behavioral problems since he entered school and was retained in Kindergarten and third grade. At the time of this evaluation, he was in fourth grade and was receiving remedial reading services, but was not in special education. Mrs. Jones also reported difficulty controlling Michael's behavior at home.

Past history showed normal development with no major illnesses or physical problems, except chronic ear infections and a minor delay in speech. At age 9, Michael was diagnosed as having Attention Deficit Disorder with Hyperactivity. Several trials on stimulant medication and then tricyclic antidepressants appeared to produce minimal effects. Medication was discontinued after one year.

Michael's mother reported significant family problems, including alcohol abuse by the father and frequent arguments at home. The parents were separated and considering divorce.

Behavior During Evaluation

Michael was friendly and cooperative throughout the evaluation. He was not unusually restless and generally showed good attention. His approach to tasks was impulsive and he was easily discouraged. Difficulties in the home and the recent separation of parents were major concerns. The results appear to be a valid sample of his present functioning.

Results

The *Wechsler Intelligence Test for Children-Revised* showed average verbal ability, very superior performance ability, and high average full-scale ability. The chances are 95 out of 100 that Michael's true IQ lies between 112 and 124. A very large difference between his average verbal IQ and very superior performance IQ was highly significant and indicative of much greater strength in nonverbal than verbal areas. Achievement testing revealed significant deficits in reading and written language, indicating learning disabilities in these areas. Mathematics achievement was generally average.

Ratings on the *Child Behavior Checklist* and related forms obtained from Michael's mother, teacher, and direct observations showed poor social competence, poor adaptive functioning in school, and behavioral/emotional problems in the clinical range for boys aged 6-11. The pattern of problems was primarily of an externalizing, aggressive nature, warranting a DSM-III-R diagnosis of Oppositional Defiant Disorder. There were also problems of hyperactivity and inattention consistent with a diagnosis of Attention Deficit-Hyperactivity Disorder, but these appeared to be less central than Michael's conduct problems, learning disabilities, and family turmoil. Psychological tests and self-ratings indicated little acknowledgement by Michael of his problems and low average self-concept. He appeared to be less amenable to individual psychotherapy than to more behavioral approaches.

Recommendations

Daily special education services for the learning disabled were recommended in the school setting, with no further grade retentions. Specific recommendations included an Individual Education Plan in reading and written language, accompanied by behavioral techniques to reinforce task completion and appropriate school behavior. Mrs. Jones was referred to a child psychologist for parent training in behavior management. Short-term counseling for Michael and either family counseling or divorce mediation were also recommended to address emotional stresses due to family instability. Evaluation of the father's alcohol abuse may also be necessary. Medication for Attention Deficit-Hyperactivity Disorder was not recommended until other interventions were in place. Evaluation by a physician for medication may be appropriate at a later date. If medication is reinstated, the effects should be carefully monitored with the Conners parent and teacher rating scales. I will continue to consult with Mrs. Jones and the school staff regarding Michael's progress.

Evaluator _____

cc: Mrs. Jones

EXAMPLE 3: SUMMARY REPORT
FOR SCHOOL

Summary reports are the most appropriate means for communicating with classroom teachers and other school staff. Since classroom teachers are mainly concerned with promoting the child's learning and social development, the summary report needs to emphasize recommendations more than details of background and results. Confidentiality is also of particular concern in the school setting, since a variety of people may have access to the report and record keeping practices vary from one school to the next. A summary report can therefore communicate pertinent information that will be useful for teachers, while protecting the confidentiality of test scores and sensitive personal and family information.

The summary report for the school should present a clear, succinct description of relevant history and major findings without giving specific IQ test scores or details of CBCL findings. Achievement test scores, on the other hand, may be useful for the teacher in planning curriculum. Recommendations should be most specific regarding the child's educational program and addressing behavioral/emotional needs in the school setting. Other recommendations for interventions outside of school should also be included in a general way, so that the teacher can be aware of the larger context of the intervention plan. Teacher support for out-of-school treatment, such as psychotherapy, is often a critical factor in motivating families to seek such help.

A comprehensive report like that presented in the first example, on the other hand, may be more appropriate for special educators who need detailed information on test scores and other findings to determine eligibility and develop an Individual Education Plan (IEP). The confidentiality of special education files is usually more stringently protected than other school records.

The following example is a summary report of Michael's comprehensive evaluation written for his classroom teachers and guidance counselor. The report briefly describes intelligence test results and behavioral/emotional functioning, but gives a more detailed outline of achievement test scores. All of the recommendations from the comprehensive report are included for Michael's educational program, so that teachers can coordinate efforts with special educators to develop his IEP and make adaptations in the mainstream classroom. Recommendations regarding behavior management and Michael's emotional needs are also included, since many of these can be applied at school as well as at home. Specific recommendations regarding strategies for psychotherapy have been excluded, along with references to alcoholism and divorce mediation. The recommendation regarding medication for Attention Deficit-Hyperactivity Disorder is retained in the summary, since any treatment along this line would concern teachers as well as parents.

SUMMARY OF EVALUATION

Re: Michael Jones
Date of birth: 11/10/75
Age: 11 years, 6 months
Grade: Fourth
Date of examination: 5/15/87

Presenting Problems and History

Michael Jones was brought for evaluation by his mother at the suggestion of Mr. Joseph Smith, Special Education Director. He had been experiencing learning and behavioral problems since he entered school and was retained in Kindergarten and third grade. At the time of this evaluation, he was in fourth grade and was receiving remedial reading services, but was not in special education. Mrs. Jones also reported difficulty controlling Michael's behavior at home and significant family problems. Mr. and Mrs. Jones were separated at the time and the children were living with Mrs. Jones.

Development was reported to be normal with no major illnesses or physical problems, except chronic ear infections and slightly delayed speech. At age 9, Michael was diagnosed as having Attention Deficit Disorder with Hyperactivity. After several trials on medication appeared to produce minimal effects, such treatment was discontinued.

Behavior During Evaluation

Michael was friendly and cooperative throughout the evaluation. He was not unusually restless and showed generally good attention. His approach to tasks was impulsive and he was easily discouraged. However, he responded well to praise and encouragement to slow down and be more careful. The results appeared to be a valid sample of his present functioning.

Test Results

The *Wechsler Intelligence Test for Children-Revised* (WISC-R) showed average verbal ability, very superior performance ability, and high average full-scale ability. A very large difference between his average verbal IQ and very superior performance IQ was highly significant and indicative of much greater strength in nonverbal than verbal areas. Individual achievement testing revealed significant deficits in reading recognition, reading comprehension, and written language, indicating learning disabilities in these areas. Mathematics achievement was generally average.

The following breakdown gives Michael's scores on the subtests of the *Peabody Individual Achievement Test* (PIAT) in grade level equivalents (GLE), percentiles, and standard scores (SS) compared to norms for his grade and age. Standard scores have a mean of 100 and standard deviation of

15. Asterisks indicate scores more than 1.5 standard deviations below his full-scale IQ on the WISC-R.

PIAT Subtest	GLE	Grade %ile	Grade SS	Age %ile	Age SS
Mathematics	7.4	82	114	51	100
Reading Recognition	3.3	18	86*	8	79*
Reading Comprehension	4.2	37	95*	17	86*
Spelling	3.5	19	87*	6	77*
General Information	5.1	55	102	28	91*

The *Test of Written Language* (TOWL) and *Test of Written Spelling* (TWS) further documented deficits in written language (Written Language Quotient = 75; Written Spelling Quotient = 77), while the *Test of Reading Comprehension* (TORC) showed exceptionally poor reading skills (Reading Comprehension Quotient = 65).

Ratings on the *Child Behavior Checklist* and related forms obtained from Michael's mother, teacher, and direct observations showed poor social competence, poor adaptive functioning in school, and behavioral/emotional problems exceeding those reported for most boys his age. The pattern of problems was primarily of an aggressive nature. There were also problems of hyperactivity and inattention, but these problems appeared to be less central than Michael's conduct problems, learning disabilities, and family stress. Psychological tests and self-ratings indicated low average self-concept and little acknowledgment by Michael of his problems.

Recommendations

Based on the present evaluation, the following recommendations are offered regarding Michael's educational program and behavioral/emotional needs.

A. Educational Program

1. Special education services for the learning disabled are recommended in the areas of reading recognition, reading comprehension, and written expression. Ideally, Michael's Individual Education Plan (IEP) should include daily services in these areas through one-to-one or small group instruction. While Michael is most eligible for special education under the learning disability category, it is important that his IEP also address behavioral/emotional needs in school.

2. No further grade retentions should be used, since Michael is already two grades behind children his age.

3. Special services in reading should be based on a multisensory approach that capitalizes on Michael's strengths in visual perception. A program organized around spelling patterns and word families would be most appropriate, utilizing visual, auditory, and kinesthetic modalities. Training in reading recognition and spelling skills should be integrated into one program if possible.

4. Instruction in reading comprehension should focus on developing both literal and inferential comprehension, organizational skills, and a better understanding of text structure and meaning. Use of visual cues could be particularly helpful, since Michael scored much higher on the PIAT reading comprehension than on the TORC, which does not use pictures. Easy reading materials (e.g., high interest-low vocabulary texts) would improve Michael's speed and fluency as well as his capacity to predict meaning in reading.

5. Michael's IEP also needs to focus on developing better writing skills. Using visual aids and outlines would be good to enhance organizational skills for writing. Exercises on a microcomputer could be particularly effective for focusing on spelling and grammatical structure, as well as organizing and editing drafts of written work.

6. Michael should remain in a mainstream classroom for math, science, and any prevocational courses. Classroom adaptations may be necessary, however, because of his problems in concentration and task completion.

7. Reading and written assignments in mainstream classes may need to be adapted by reducing their length and the amount of material presented at one time. Short, frequent assignments in an orderly sequence are preferable to long-term projects. Easy reading materials may also be necessary to adapt to Michael's learning disability. Clear, concise outlines of daily assignments are important for enhancing his organizational skills.

8. A check and point system is recommended to reinforce on-task behavior and completion of assignments and to reduce aggressive, noncompliant behavior in school. This could consist of a simple daily recording form on which the teacher can check whether Michael completed assigned work in each subject and award points for specified behaviors, such as staying in his seat, raising his hand for assistance, and working quietly. The system should begin with modest, well-defined daily and weekly goals tied to a menu of rewards. The goals can be gradually increased as his productivity improves. A similar system could be developed to reduce aggressive behavior during recess and less structured time.

9. Training in self-monitoring strategies and study skills is recommended to improve on-task behavior and work completion, along with the check and point system outlined above. Positive reinforcement for slowing down and working carefully has already proven effective with Michael. Frequent verbal repetition of expectations and consequences would also be helpful.

10. Early enrollment in a vocationally-oriented program is recommended to improve Michael's motivation and to capitalize on his cognitive strengths in visual-spatial areas.

B. Behavior Management and Emotional Needs

1. Time-outs, loss of privileges, and behavioral contracts are the best approaches for managing Michael's behavior. Continuation of the recent behavioral contract developed at school is recommended.

2. Training in social problem-solving skills is also recommended for Michael. The program should focus on defining social problems, generating alternative solutions, evaluating consequences, and developing and modeling more socially appropriate behavior. Focusing on how to respond to name-calling would be a good starting point, since this has been a particular problem for Michael leading to confrontations with peers.

3. To develop better social competence, Michael needs to be more involved in social organizations and structured social activities. Enrollment in a summer camp designed for troubled children would be a good immediate opportunity. Participation in a Big Brother program could provide a positive male role model for him. Participation in team sports, YMCA programs, and other organized activities are further examples.

4. Participation in a peer tutoring situation at school would provide an additional opportunity for Michael to develop better social relations. The best approach might be to have Michael tutor another child in an area of his strength, such as math, thereby enhancing his self-esteem and sense of social responsibility.

5. Michael's parents need to recognize that family issues and conflict are major factors influencing Michael's behavior. Stability and consistency in the home are necessary for any long-term improvements in his behavior. Michael and his parents have been referred for counseling to address behavior management and family issues.

6. Michael's learning disabilities and family problems suggest that Attention Deficit-Hyperactivity Disorder is not the primary cause of his behavior and learning problems.

Although Michael displays some of the characteristics of Attention Deficit-Hyperactivity Disorder, this appears to be less central than other concerns outlined above. Medication is not recommended without other interventions. Once the interventions outlined above are in place, further evaluation by a physician for medication may be warranted. If medication is reinstated, Michael's behavior should be carefully monitored with regular reports from parents and teachers. One approach is to have parents and teachers complete the Conners rating scales weekly and chart the results concurrently with changes in the dosage.

7. A follow-up assessment with the CBCL/4-16, TRF, and YSR is recommended in about one year to evaluate the effects of interventions.

Evaluator_____

cc: Mrs. Jones
Mr. Joseph Smith, Special Education Director

SUMMARY

The written report is an important component of assessment, often serving as the main vehicle for integrating findings, formulating conclusions, and communicating recommendations. This chapter illustrated how the results of empirically-based assessment can be combined with information from other sources in reports intended for different consumers, including a comprehensive report for parents who have requested an evaluation and professionals closely involved in a case; a briefer summary report for practitioners who are not closely involved with the evaluation; and a summary report for school personnel.

Chapter 9
Forensic Reports Involving Empirically-Based Assessment

Forensic reports represent a special application of the assessment process geared toward litigation and court proceedings. Forensic evaluations of children are often necessitated by civil, juvenile, or family law matters, such as custody disputes, parental rights, juvenile dispositions, and abuse and neglect charges. Forensic evaluations can be requested by parents, attorneys representing different parties involved in the case, victims' advocates, schools, state agencies, or courts. Such evaluations can address children's cognitive, behavioral, and emotional functioning, parental fitness, conditions in the home, support systems for the family, or detailed accounts of actual events involved in criminal allegations such as abuse.

Forensic evaluations employ many different formats depending on the nature of the questions addressed and the number of evaluators involved. Because forensic evaluations often involve assessment of multiple parties, a forensic team of two or more practitioners may conduct the evaluation and then combine results in a team report. In the team approach, one person is usually designated as the primary evaluator and others as secondary evaluators. An alternative approach is for one practitioner to conduct the entire evaluation, writing separate reports on each party and then producing a summary of conclusions and recommendations. In either approach, the primary evaluator usually testifies as an expert witness in court to discuss the specific findings and recommendations contained in the report.

EXAMPLE: A CHILD FORENSIC EVALUATION

This chapter illustrates how empirically-based assessment can be integrated into a child forensic evaluation. The example we have chosen concerns two children involved in a parental custody dispute. The full evaluation involved assessment of both children and both parents. Assessment of the children utilized cognitive tests, semi-structured clinical interviews, behavioral observations in family sessions, and ratings by their parents on the Minnesota Child Development Inventory and the Child Behavior Checklist. Assessment of the parents utilized personality tests, rating scales covering parenting skills and attitudes, observations of their behavior in family sessions, reviews of medical, psychological, and legal records, and interviews. Their responses on the Child Behavior Checklist were used to structure questioning regarding their concerns about the children, approaches to discipline, and other aspects of parenting.

We have confined our example to the evaluation report on the children in order to highlight the results of the empirically-based measures and interpretations that are especially appropriate for this type of report. Special consideration is given to the differences in the parents' perspectives on their children's functioning and technical data on the validity of the results. To protect confidentiality, we have used fictitious names and omitted the family history and evaluation of the parents. We have also omitted the summary report and recommendations regarding custody, since these, of course, would be based on the results of the full evaluation.

CHILD EVALUATION REPORT

Name: Stephen Collins   Name: Melanie Collins
Date of birth: 2/25/83   Date of birth: 10/1/84
Age: 4 years, 7 months   Age: 3 years, 0 months
Date of examination: 10/8/87

Reason for Referral

This portion of the evaluation is to assess each child's cognitive capacity, developmental functioning, and behavioral/emotional problems. The children are presently in the custody of both parents under a temporary order by the court. They spend half the week with each parent.

Assessment Procedures

McCarthy Scales of Children's Abilities

Minnesota Child Development Inventory (MCDI; completed by each parent)

Child Behavior Checklist/4-16 (CBCL/4-16; completed by each parent)

Child Behavior Checklist/2-3 (CBCL/2-3; completed by each parent)

Semi-structured clinical interviews with each child

Behavior observations during family sessions

Interviews with each parent separately (The family history is contained in reports regarding the parents. Information presented here covers the parents' reports on each child's developmental history and current problems.)

Stephen Collins

Background Information. Stephen's mother reported that he was the product of a normal pregnancy and showed normal language and motor development. Both parents acknowledged that Stephen was aggressive and difficult to discipline. The mother reported difficulty with toilet training, stating that Stephen wets the bed at least one night a week and soils during the day about once a month. Mrs. Collins stressed that Stephen's problems had intensified since the parents separated one year ago, while Mr. Collins stated that the problems had decreased. Mrs. Collins expressed particular concern about Stephen's behavior toward his sister, Melanie. She stated that he often physically attacks his sister and has engaged in "sex play" with her, such as kissing her on the mouth and lying on top of her. Mr. Collins, on the other hand, reported no unusual aggressive or sexual behavior. Mrs. Collins believed that Stephen's behavior was a result of imitating his father, while Mr. Collins felt that Stephen's behavior was a reaction to adjustment problems and the many transitions he was experiencing.

Behavior During Evaluation. Stephen was cooperative and obedient throughout the testing session, though somewhat distracted and inattentive. He was very active and displayed much curiosity, often leaving his seat during testing and asking questions about objects in the room. His conversation was appropriate for his age, though test questions often had to be repeated when he was distracted by other things. The test scores appear to give a valid indication of his current cognitive functioning.

During the semi-structured clinical interview, Stephen displayed a generally aggressive approach to social problem-solving, such as stating that he would grab a toy he wanted from another child and that he would hit someone smaller who tried to fight with him. However, he did seem to have an age-appropriate sense of rules. He expressed sadness and anger about his parents' separation and was ambivalent about whom he wanted to live with. He expressed more affection toward his mother than his father, and stated that his father hits his mother. His drawing of his family, however, showed both parents together with himself and his sister. Stephen responded negatively to all questions regarding sexual behavior by adults toward him or his witnessing adult sexual behavior, though he appeared upset by these questions.

After individual testing and interviewing, Stephen was observed in family sessions first with his sister and father, and then with his sister and mother. Stephen displayed much independence, tending to play by himself most of the time regardless of which parent was present. He displayed minimal affect toward both his parents and sister. He ignored his father during most of their time together, except when his father made direct attempts to build things with him. With his mother, Stephen occasionally reached out to request help with building toys or to show her something he had made, but otherwise played by himself. He did not attempt to include his sister in any games and ignored her verbal comments to him. At the end of the session, Stephen refused to put the toys away and ignored his mother's statements that it was time to leave, until she physically removed him from the room.

Test Results. The *McCarthy Scales of Children's Abilities* measure cognitive functioning in children 2 to 8 years of age. Stephen showed ability in the superior range, with a General Cognitive Index of 120. (Scores between 90 and 109 are considered to be in the average range on the McCarthy scales.) Stephen's GCI was equivalent to a General Cognitive Age of 5 1/2 years, as defined by Kaufman and Kaufman (1977). Stephen scored above average on scales measuring verbal skills, perceptual performance, and motor skills, and average on scales measuring quantitative and memory skills. The following breakdown gives Stephen's Scale Index scores on the five McCarthy Scales, each having an average score of 50 and standard deviation of 10:

Scale	Scale Index
Verbal	60
Perceptual-Performance	68
Quantitative	55
Memory	48
Motor	60

The *Minnesota Child Development Inventory* (MCDI) was completed by each parent separately to obtain their perspectives on Stephen's general development. The MCDI is a 320-item rating scale on which a parent answers "yes" or "no" to each statement that describes the child's present or past behavior. Items cover typical developmental behaviors for children aged 6 months to 6 years-3 months. Stephen's parents showed general agreement that his development was within the normal range or higher on all scales except the one measuring personal-social skills. His age equivalent score for general development was 5 years-8 months on his mother's ratings and 5 years-9 months on his father's ratings, which was consistent with his general cognitive age of 5 1/2 years on the McCarthy Scales. On the Personal-Social scale, the father scored Stephen at a higher level of development than did the mother. However, it should be noted that the age equivalents yielded by the Personal-Social scale are of dubious validity above age 3, so that Stephen's scores may not reflect a true difference in the parents' perspectives in this area. The following breakdown gives the age equivalent scores (years-months) for the ratings by mother and father on the MCDI scales:

Scale	Mother	Father
General Development	5-8	5-9
Gross Motor	5-9	5-9
Fine Motor	6-3*	6-3*
Expressive Language	6-3*	6-3*
Comprehension-Conceptual	6-0	6-3*
Situation Comprehension	4-3	4-3
Self Help	4-6	4-9
Personal-Social	3-9	6-3*

*ceiling score

The *Child Behavior Checklist/4-16 (CBCL/4-16)* was completed by each parent separately to gain their perspectives on Stephen's social competence and behavior problems. The CBCL/4-16 is a standardized rating scale containing 20 social competence and 118 behavior problems items. Parents provide information on their child's activities, involvement in social organizations, social relations, and school performance. They then rate their child on each problem, using a 0-1-2 scale for how true the item is of the child now or within the past 6 months. Their responses are scored on three competence scales and a variety of problem scales and are compared to norms for the child's sex/age group.

There was a striking contrast between scores on Stephen's CBCL/4-16 completed by his mother and father. Ratings of Stephen by his *mother* produced a total competence score of 13.0, which fell in the normal range compared to norms for parents' ratings of boys aged 4-5 years (>10th percentile). The score on the Activities scale was well within the normal range, while the score on the Social scale (5th percentile) was just above the clinical cutoff at the 2nd percentile. The mother listed several sports and activities, as well as chores at home. She also reported participation in pre-school and two or three friends that Stephen played with once or twice a week. However, the mother rated Stephen's behavior worse than other children his age with his sister, other children, and his parents. Stephen's total problem score of 98 from the mother's ratings was well above the cutoff of 42 on norms for boys aged 4-5, thus falling in the clinical range (>90th percentile). Both his Internalizing and Externalizing scores were in the clinical range (>90th percentile), as were scores on 6 out of 8 narrow-band syndrome scales (>98th percentile): the Social Withdrawal, Depressed, Sex Problems, Schizoid, Aggressive, and Delinquent scales. Figure 9-1 illustrates the computer-scored profile of the mother's ratings of Stephen on the CBCL/4-16 problem scales that served as Exhibit A to the court.

The *mother's* ratings on the Social Withdrawal scale included scores for 9 out of 12 items, such as, *18. Deliberately harms self* (mother crossed out "attempts suicide"); *65. Refuses to talk*; and *111. Withdrawn, doesn't get involved with other children.* The Depressed scale included scores for 19 out of 25 items, such as *9. Can't get his mind off certain thoughts, obsessions* (mother wrote in "killing, hurting"); *35. Feels worthless or inferior*; *47. Nightmares*; *52. Feels guilty*; and *103. Unhappy, sad, or depressed.* The Sex Problems scale included scores on 4 out of 6 items, including *31. Fears he might think or do something bad*; *59. Plays with own sex parts in public*; *60. Plays with own sex parts too much*; and *73. Sexual problems* (mother wrote in "sexual with sister, mother"). The Schizoid scale included scores for "very true or often true" on 3 out of 9 items,

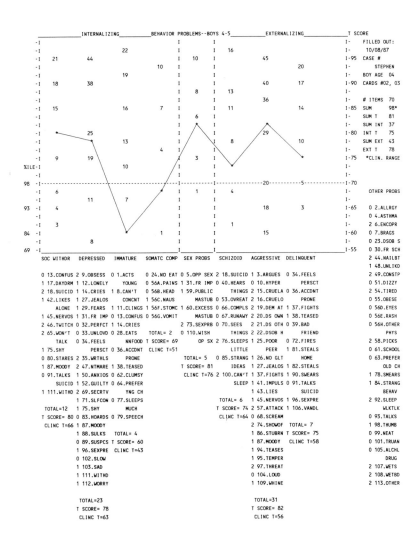

Figure 9-1. Computer-scored version of the CBCL/4-16 problem scales for mother's ratings of 4-year-old Stephen.

including *76. Sleeps less than most children*; *100. Trouble sleeping* (mother wrote in "afraid, nightmares"), and item *18* described above. The Aggressive scale included scores for 22 out of 25 items, while the Delinquent scale included 7 out of 12 items. These latter two scales included scores for arguing, cruelty, destructiveness, disobedience, temper tantrums, stealing at home and outside the home, thinking about sex too much, and a variety of other problems related to physical and verbal aggression. The overall pattern of Stephen's problems was highly similar to the Sex Problems profile type obtained for clinically referred boys aged 4-5, as indicated by an intraclass correlation of .721. (An ICC of .721 is comparable to a Pearson correlation of approximately .93 according to Achenbach and Edelbrock, 1983.)

Ratings on the CBCL/4-16 by Stephen's *father* produced a total competence score of 7.0, which fell within the clinical range on norms for boys aged 4-5 (<10th percentile), in contrast to the mother's score in the normal range. Scores on both the Activities and Social scales (5th percentile) were just above the 2nd percentile clinical cutoff. The father reported that Stephen participated in only one sport and two activities and had no chores at home. He also reported participation in preschool and contacts with one or two friends. He rated Stephen's behavior as the same as other children his age in terms of getting along with his sister, other children, and parents. Stephen's total problem score of 17 from the father's ratings was well within the normal range for boys aged 4-5, in sharp contrast to the high problem score obtained from the mother. The father scored Stephen on only 17 out of 118 problem items, such as those concerning shyness, preferring younger children, strange ideas (father wrote in "normal child fantasies"), threatening people, and problems wetting self during the day and night. Figure 9-2 illustrates the computer-scored profile of the father's ratings of Stephen on the CBCL problem scales that served as Exhibit B to the court.

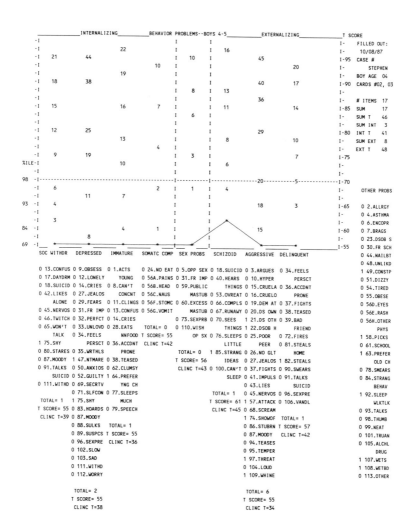

Figure 9-2. Computer-scored version of the CBCL/4-16 problem scales for father's ratings of 4-year-old Stephen.

Melanie Collins

Background Information. Mrs. Collins reported that Melanie was born one month early in a normal delivery. She has shown normal language and motor development, but has always been a moody child, according to her mother. She has sometimes been difficult to discipline and alternates between being aggressive and withdrawn. Mrs. Collins said Melanie also has "sick spells" about once a month, involving an upset stomach and occasional vomiting. Mrs. Collins said the pediatrician has not been able to identify any illness causing these problems. Mrs. Collins also expressed concern about Melanie's "strange sexual behavior" similar to what she had described for Stephen. Mr. Collins agreed that Melanie had stomachaches, but said these seldom occurred at his house. He described Melanie as a pleasant, quiet child, who presented no special management problems. He reported that she got along well with her brother, with him, and with his girlfriend.

Behavior During Evaluation. Melanie was pleasant and cooperative throughout the session. She completed all tasks willingly, showing good attention and positive affect. The test scores appear to give a valid indication of her current cognitive functioning.

In the semi-structured clinical interview, Melanie answered questions about interpersonal and family situations in a manner typical for children her age. She demonstrated no unusual thought patterns or strange emotional reactions. She said she loves her mother more than her dad, but also said she loves her dad. When asked about sleep problems, Melanie said she was afraid of the dark and that "someone might come in," but did not name a particular person. She responded negatively to all questions regarding sexual behavior by adults toward her or witnessing adult sexual behavior.

Following individual testing and interviewing, Melanie was observed in family sessions first with her brother and father, and then with her brother and mother. She played by herself at first using several different toys in the room. Her behavior and affect toward her father fluctuated from initially being quite cool and distant and then becoming more relaxed and extremely affectionate. At the end of the time with her father, she hugged and kissed him several times. Melanie's behavior with her mother was much more task oriented. Typically, her mother would demonstrate a task or simple game and then Melanie would imitate her and perform on her own. Her affect toward her mother was neutral at first and then more loving at the end. Interaction between Melanie and her brother was minimal, as both children played their own games and approached parents separately. Melanie appeared disappointed when told that her time was finished and sat passively watching while her mother attempted to remove Stephen from the room.

Test Results. Cognitive testing with the *McCarthy Scales of Children's Abilities* showed ability in the superior range, with a General Cognitive Index of 127, which was equivalent to a General Cognitive Age of 4 years, as defined by Kaufman and Kaufman (1977). Melanie scored above average on scales measuring verbal skills, perceptual performance, and motor skills, and average on scales measuring quantitative and memory skills. The following breakdown gives Melanie's Scale Index scores on the five McCarthy Scales, each having an average score of 50 and standard deviation of 10:

Scale	Scale Index
Verbal	69
Perceptual-Performance	62
Quantitative	59
Memory	71
Motor	62

The *Minnesota Child Development Inventory* (MCDI) was completed by each parent separately to obtain their perspectives on Melanie's general development. Melanie's parents showed general agreement that her development was within the normal range or higher on all scales. Her age equivalent score for general development was 3 years-8 months on both her mother's and father's ratings, which was consistent with her general cognitive age of 4 years on the McCarthy Scales. On the Expressive Language scale, her mother scored Melanie at a higher level of development than did her father. However, it should be noted that the age equivalents for the Expressive Language scale have dubious validity above age 3, so that Melanie's scores may not reflect a true difference in the parents' perceptions in this area. The following breakdown gives the age equivalent scores (years-months) for the ratings by mother and father on the MCDI scales:

Scale	Mother	Father
General Development	3-8	3-8
Gross Motor	4-6	3-9
Fine Motor	3-8	3-8
Expressive Language	6-3*	3-8
Comprehension-Conceptual	4-5	3-8
Situation Comprehension	3-6	4-0
Self Help	3-0	4-3
Personal-Social	3-9	3-9
*ceiling score		

The *Child Behavior Checklist/2-3* (CBCL/2-3) was completed by each parent separately to gain their perspectives on Melanie's behavior problems. The CBCL/2-3 is a standardized rating scale similar to the CBCL/4-16, but designed for children aged 2-3 years. Parents rate their child on 99 problems, using a 0-1-2 scale for how true the item is now or within the past 2 months. There are no social competence items on the CBCL/2-3.

There was a striking contrast in the results obtained on Melanie's CBCL/2-3 from the two parents. The *mother's* ratings on the CBCL/2-3 produced a total problem score of 69, which was above the clinical cutoff of 63, thus falling in the clinical range (>90th percentile) on norms for parents' ratings of boys and girls aged 2-3 years. Melanie's Internalizing score was also in the clinical range (>90th percentile), while her

Externalizing score was in the normal range. Scores on the Depressed and Sleep Problems syndrome scales were in the clinical range (>98th percentile). The Depressed scale included scores for 11 out of 15 items, including *21. Disturbed by any change in routine*; *25. Doesn't get along with other children*; *28. Doesn't want to go out of home*; *43. Looks unhappy without good reason*; *77. Stares into space or seems preoccupied*; *80. Strange behavior* ("sexual behavior" written in); *82. Sudden changes in mood or feelings*; *83. Sulks a lot*; *90. Unhappy, sad, or depressed*; *98. Withdrawn, doesn't get involved with others*; and *99. Worrying*. The Sleep Problems scale included scores for all 8 items, most of which were scored as "very true or often true": *22. Doesn't want to sleep alone*; *38. Has trouble getting to sleep*; *48. Nightmares*; *50. Overtired*; *64. Resists going to bed at night*; *74. Sleeps less than most children during the day and/or night*; *84. Talks or cries out in sleep*; and *94. Wakes up often at night*. Scores on the four other syndrome scales were in the normal range, though the mother did score *45. Nausea, feels sick (without medical cause)* and *78. Stomachaches or cramps (without medical cause)* on the Somatic Problems scale. Figure 9-3 illustrates the computer-scored profile of the mother's ratings of Melanie on the CBCL/2-3 that served as Exhibit C to the court.

Ratings on the CBCL/2-3 by Melanie's *father* produced a total problem score of 32, which was well below the clinical cutoff of 63, thus falling in the normal range. Scores on the Internalizing and Externalizing scales were also in the normal range, as were scores on all eight of the syndrome scales. The father scored only 32 out of 99 problem items, indicating only occasional problems, such as clinging, shyness, upset with changes, nightmares, resisting going to bed, destroying others' things, refusing to eat, stubbornness, temper tantrums, and uncooperativeness. Figure 9-4 illustrates the computer-scored version of the father's ratings of Melanie on the CBCL/2-3 that served as Exhibit D to the court.

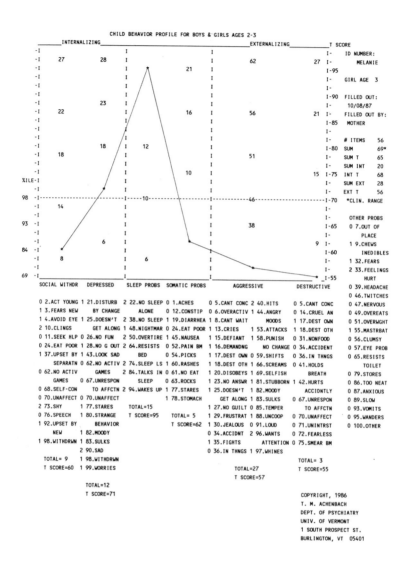

Figure 9-3. Computer-scored version of the CBCL/2-3 problem scales for mother's ratings of 3-year-old Melanie.

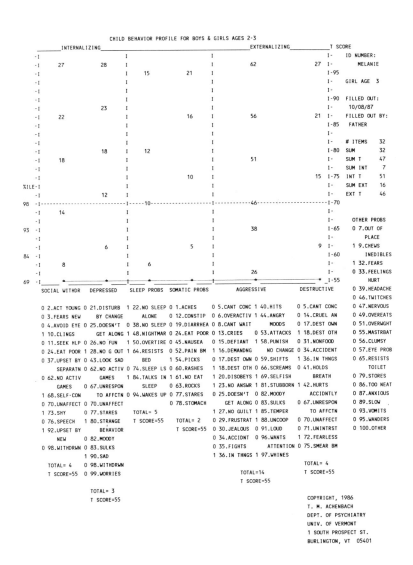

Figure 9-4. Computer-scored version of the CBCL/2-3 problem scales for father's ratings of 3-year-old Melanie.

Summary of Findings

The results of this evaluation indicate that both children have above average intelligence with no significant cognitive deficits. Their verbal and performance skills are well developed for their age. The parents' ratings of the children's developmental skills produced scores approximately one year above Stephen's chronological age and 8 months above Melanie's chronological age, consistent with their above average cognitive test scores. The parents differed in ratings regarding Stephen's personal-social skills and Melanie's expressive language, but neither rated these below average. With such high cognitive and developmental functioning, both children were able to participate appropriately in all aspects of the evaluation and gave competent responses within normal expectations for their ages.

The parents gave strikingly different reports of the children's behavior problems, with the mother reporting problems in the clinical range for both Stephen and Melanie, while the father reported problems in the normal range. The mother's ratings of Stephen on the CBCL/4-16 indicated problems of both an internalizing and externalizing nature well beyond levels normally expected for 4-5-year-old boys. She reported problems related to social withdrawal, depression, aggression, and "delinquent" behavior (stealing, vandalism), as well as sleep problems and enuresis. Stephen's very high score on the Sex Problems scale and the high correlation with the Sex Problems profile type are of particular concern, since the sexual behaviors reported by Mrs. Collins are highly unusual for boys of his age. The mother's ratings of Melanie on the CBCL/2-3 also indicated serious problems well beyond levels normally expected for 2-3-year-old children. Melanie's problems appear to be more of an internalizing nature, involving depression and sleep problems. Her frequent stomachaches and sleep problems are indicative of significant anxiety and stress. These results indicate that, according to their mother, both children are exhibiting severe emotional and behavioral problems in the context of the family breakup and conflict between their parents.

Though neither Stephen nor Melanie reported any incidents of adult sexual behavior toward them in this evaluation, the possibility of sexual abuse of both children warrants further investigation.

The fact that the parents generally agreed on ratings of the children's developmental skills makes the difference in their ratings of behavior problems all the more dramatic. Since the average correlation for interparent agreement on the CBCL/4-16 total problem score is quite high, ($r = .75$ for boys aged 4-5; Achenbach & Edelbrock; 1983), the difference between the two parents' reports is an important fact to consider in a custody decision. It is possible that the mother may overestimate the severity of problems, at least for her son. Stephen's total problem score of 98 was above the average of 59.8 for clinically-referred boys aged 4-5 (Achenbach & Edelbrock, 1983), while Melanie's total problem score of 69 was close to the average of 70.5 for clinically-referred boys and girls aged 2-3 (Achenbach, Edelbrock, & Howell, 1987). The father, on the other hand, may underestimate the severity of problems for both children, since his CBCLs produced scores below the average total scores obtained for the normative samples. Stephen's total problem score of 17 was below the average of 24.1 for the normative sample of boys aged 4-5, while Melanie's total problem score of 32 was below the average of 40.6 for the normative sample of children aged 2-3.

It is also very likely that the children's behavior does indeed vary across the different situations with their parents, with problems becoming more pronounced in the mother's presence. Since the children seem to be attached to both parents, regular visits with the noncustodial parent are recommended, assuming that no abuse by a parent is uncovered in further evaluation. The children could also benefit from short term expressive therapy to help in their emotional adjustment to the divorce and custody arrangement.

Evaluator _____

Exhibit A: CBCL/4-16 profile of mother's ratings of Stephen

Exhibit B: CBCL/4-16 profile of father's ratings of Stephen
Exhibit C: CBCL/2-3 profile of mother's ratings of Melanie
Exhibit D: CBCL/2-3 profile of father's ratings of Melanie

SUMMARY

This chapter illustrated the use of the Child Behavior Checklist in conjunction with other procedures as part of a forensic evaluation of 3- and 4-year-old siblings necessitated by a parental custody dispute. Both parents completed the CBCL and Minnesota Child Development Inventory. The children were interviewed, were observed in play sessions with each parent, and were administered the McCarthy Scales of Children's Abilities. Although the parents' ratings on the Minnesota Child Development Inventory agreed well with each other and with the McCarthy scores, their very different ratings on the CBCL revealed major discrepancies between their views of the children's behavioral/emotional functioning that were not evident in any other source of data.

The much higher problem scores on the CBCLs completed by the mother than on those completed by the father appeared to indicate both a higher rate of problem behavior when the children were with the mother and the father's tendency to understate problems. Recommendations for therapy for the children were based on evaluation of the children. A high score on the Sex Problems scale and a high correlation with the Sex Problems profile type also suggested sexual abuse that should be investigated further. Recommendations regarding custody and visitation rights, as well as any mental health services for the parents, were not included in our case example, since these would be based on the complete forensic evaluations of both parents, as well as the children.

Chapter 10
Answers to Commonly Asked Questions

This chapter addresses questions that occasionally arise about the forms of the CBCL and the relations between them. Some of the questions are answered in more detail elsewhere in this *Guide* or in the *Manual* for a particular instrument. The questions are grouped according to whether they pertain to the instruments in general or to comparisons between instruments. If you have a question that is not found under one heading, look under the other heading. The Table of Contents, Index, *Manuals*, and the book by Achenbach and McConaughy (1987) may also help you find answers to questions not listed here.

GENERAL QUESTIONS

1. Why don't the total problem scores correspond to the item numbers on some forms? For example, the CBCL and TRF are said to have 118 problem items and maximum total problem scores of 240, but the highest item number is 113.

Answer: Item *56* on the CBCL and TRF includes seven specific physical complaints designated as *a* through *g*. Combined with the remaining 111 specifically stated problems, this sums to 118 problem items. In addition, item *56h* provides space for the respondent to enter physical problems not otherwise listed and item *113* provides three spaces for respondents to enter additional problems of any sort. Total problem scores are computed as the sum of 1s and 2s for the 118 specific problems + item *56h* + the highest score the respondent gives to any additional problems written in for item *113*. If a 2 is scored for all 118 items, *56h*, and *113*, the total score would be 240.

2. Can't social desirability, lying, and other rater characteristics such as depression bias scores on the rating forms?

Answer: Many rater characteristics may be associated with scores on forms such as the CBCL, TRF, and YSR. Research has shown, for example, that mothers' self-reported depression on the Beck Depression Inventory correlates significantly with their ratings of their children's problems on the CBCL (Friedlander, Weiss, & Traylor, 1986). Some have interpreted this association as indicating a "biasing" effect of maternal depression on ratings of behavior problems. However, the correlation between mothers' self-ratings and their ratings of their children might mean that children with numerous problems make their mothers unhappy. The correlation might also reflect adverse reactions by the mothers and their children to some common factor, such as environmental stress or a shared genetic vulnerability. Whatever the correct interpretation, Friedlander et al. also found that CBCL scores still discriminated significantly between psychiatric and pediatric referrals, even after the effects of maternal depression scores were partialled out. However, the most important point is this: Associations between raters' characteristics and scores for the children they rate may or may not involve biases, but there is no way to be absolutely certain in every case. Instead, it is necessary to compare multiple sources of data in order to avoid basing conclusions on too limited or unrepresentative sample of data about a child.

3. Why are there no norms or standard scores for the "Other Problems" listed on each profile?

Answer: The "Other Problems" listed on each profile do not constitute a scale. They are merely the items that were too rarely reported for a particular sex/age group to be included in the factor analysis for that group and those items that did not load highly enough on any factor to be part of a scale for a particular sex/age group. We thus found no associations among the "Other Problems" to warrant treating them as a scale. However, any of these items reported for a child may be important in its own right and is counted toward the total problem score.

4. What if there are disagreements between scores obtained from two informants of the same type, such as two parents or two teachers?

Answer: Disagreements–even between informants who play similar roles with respect to a child–can be as informative as agreements. Although small to moderate discrepancies between similar informants are not uncommon, a large discrepancy in profile pattern or elevation is worth investigating with the informants. In some cases, it may reflect differences in the samples of the child's behavior to which the informants are exposed. Some behaviors may be displayed only in the mother's presence, for example, while others may be displayed only in the father's presence. Or one parent may evoke certain behaviors, while the other one does not. Or one parent may have less tolerance or be more sensitive to certain behaviors than the other is. On the average, the scores on CBCLs completed by mothers do not differ significantly from those completed by fathers. A large discrepancy between a particular mother and father should therefore not be blamed on differing response tendencies of mothers versus fathers in general, but should be investigated to determine the reason for the discrepancy between this particular mother and father. By the same token, major discrepancies between profiles from ratings by teachers who have a child in different classes should prompt the user to explore whether the child's behavior is markedly different in the two classes, whether the teachers interact differently with the child, or whether they have very different standards of judgment.

5. What if a parent or adolescent can't read well enough to complete the CBCL or YSR?

Answer: If a respondent's reading skills are known to be below the 5th grade level, the CBCL or YSR can be read aloud by an interviewer who writes down the answers. If the respondent's reading skills are questionable, a copy of the form can be handed to him/her by an interviewer who retains a second copy and says: "I'm going to read the questions on this form and I'll write down your answers." Most respondents who can read adequately will soon start answering the questions before the interviewer reads them, but this procedure avoids embarrassment for those who cannot read well. If a form is administered orally, it should be done in a private location, out of earshot of others.

6. What if a respondent can't read English but can read another language?

Answer: At this writing, we know of translations of the CBCL into 24 languages. Write to Dr. Achenbach for the current status of translations of each form.

7. How are interpretations of the profiles made?

Answer: The profiles scored from each instrument provide standardized summaries of a child's characteristics as seen by the person completing the instrument and compared to norms for reports by similar informants. Because each type of informant is exposed to different samples of the child's functioning and may apply different standards of judgment, none of the profiles should be interpreted in isolation from other data about the child. Rather than being "interpreted" like a projective test, data from a profile should be compared and integrated with other types of data about the child, such as profiles scored from reports by other informants, developmental history, tests, biomedical data, and clinical interviews. The integration of multiple types of data should aim to highlight both the similarities and differences in functioning across different contexts and to tailor interventions to each of the contexts in which help is needed. Achenbach and McConaughy (1987) illustrate integration of multiaxial data for a variety of cases.

8. Can projectives, other personality tests, and family assessment be used with the CBCL and related materials?

Answer: Our empirically-based assessment procedures can be used with any other assessment approach. Although our multiaxial assessment model focuses on the child as seen from different perspectives using standardized, normed, and empirically-based procedures whenever possible, it does not preclude using unstandardized measures or assessment of other important areas, such as family systems.

9. How can the profiles be used in making administrative categorizations, such as DSM diagnoses required for third party payments and determination of special education eligibility according to Public Law 94-142?

Answer: Patterns of strengths and deficits revealed by the profiles, as well as scores on individual scales, provide empirical documentation required for administrative categorizations such as those involved in DSM diagnoses and determination of special education eligibility. If a child is achieving well below the level expected on the basis of ability tests and has high scores on the Depressed scale of the CBCL, TRF, YSR, and/or DOF, for example, this would support a DSM-III-R diagnosis of Depression or Dysthymia and a determination of serious emotional disturbance based on the P.L. 94-142 criterion of a pervasive mood of unhappiness severe enough to affect school functioning. Strong relations between CBCL scale scores and DSM diagnoses have been demonstrated in a study by Edelbrock and Costello (1988), while applications of the profiles to DSM diagnoses and P.L. 94-142 have been extensively illustrated in the book by Achenbach and McConaughy (1987), as well as in the examples of reports in Chapter 8 of the present book.

COMPARISONS BETWEEN INSTRUMENTS

1. Why do items differ from one instrument to another?

Answer: Although many problem items are quite similar across all the instruments, each instrument is geared to the type of informant and the context in which that informant sees the child. The TRF, for example, omits the CBCL item pertaining to nightmares, whereas the CBCL omits the TRF item regarding disruption of class discipline. The reproductions of the CBCL/2-3, TRF, YSR, and DOF in Chapters 4-7 indicate the overlap among forms. The forms differ more with respect to competence items than problem items. Neither the CBCL/2-3 nor the DOF have competence items, because of the difficulty of assessing competence for 2-3-year-olds and during 10-minute observations of behavior.

2. Why do syndrome scales differ from one profile to another?

Answer: The syndrome scales were constructed by determining which problems tended to co-occur in ratings of clinical samples of a particular sex/age group by a particular type of respondent. The syndrome scales vary from one profile to another, because of differences between items from one form of the CBCL to another and because of variations between the syndromes found in ratings of different sex/age groups by different informants. Even where the items of a syndrome are similar for two or more groups, the percentiles and standard scores may differ, reflecting variations between the distributions of problems in different groups. It is therefore important to score children on the profile appropriate for their sex and age.

3. Why do syndrome scales having similar names differ in their locations on different profiles?

Answer: Syndrome scales are arranged from left to right on each profile according to the way in which the scales were found to group together in "second-order" factor analyses, as detailed in the *Manuals* for each instrument. The left-most scale on the profile for each sex/age group is the most extreme Internalizing scale for that group, whereas the right-most scale is the most extreme Externalizing scale for that group. The scales found to form the Internalizing and Externalizing groupings and their orders within those groupings differ somewhat from one sex/age group to another.

4. Why do the scoring profiles for the CBCL/4-16, TRF, YSR, and DOF span different age ranges?

Answer: The CBCL/4-16 and TRF both have profiles that span ages 6-11 and 12-16, but TRF profiles were not constructed below age 6, because few children are in academic school classes before the age of 6. The YSR was constructed to span ages 11 to 18, because this included the youngest age at which most youth are able to complete it and the oldest age for which most of the items remain appropriate and for which representative normative samples could be obtained. If a user wishes to compare YSR findings for 17- to 18-year-olds with CBCL or TRF findings, and adequate parent or teacher informants are available, the CBCL and TRF can be scored on their 12-16-year profiles. Even though norms were not sought above age 16 for these instruments, they can be used to make descriptive comparisons of 17- and 18-year-olds. Geared mainly to elementary and middle school settings, the DOF normative data are based on ages 5 to 14. However, comparisons between the target child and other children in the same setting can be made for any age and are often more helpful than age norms for direct observations.

5. Why do the rating intervals for the problem items differ among the instruments?

Answer: The CBCL/4-16 and YSR specify that ratings should be based on the preceding 6 months in order to pick up low frequency but memorable events important for clinical assessment, such as suicidal behavior, firesetting, and running away from home. The TRF specifies that ratings be based on the preceding 2 months, because longer rating periods would reduce the portion of the school year during which ratings could be made and because teachers are not apt to remember the specific behaviors of individual childen over longer periods. If a user wishes to base CBCL/4-16, YSR, and TRF ratings on exactly the same periods, the CBCL and YSR instructions can be changed to request the same rating period as on the TRF. Shortening the CBCL/4-16 and YSR rating periods seldom has much effect on scale scores, because relatively few items are likely to be scored solely on the basis of events occurring several months previously. The CBCL/2-3 specifies a 2-month rating period, because the behavior of 2-3-year-olds changes quickly enough that longer rating periods are less likely to reflect their current functioning. The orientation of the DOF differs from that of the other instruments, in that it obtains a sample of behavior over a brief, precisely defined interval, instead of judgments by informants from memory over relatively long periods. The DOF's 10-minute rating period is designed to sample what is actually observed during an interval that can be adequately representative when repeated and averaged over three to six occasions.

6. What about the small differences in wording and scoring instructions for items that are considered similar on the different instruments?

Answer: We designed each instrument to optimize its use by the intended respondents, even if it required different wording for similar items on the different instruments. An example is problem item 9, which is *Can't get his/her mind off certain thoughts; obessions (describe)* on the CBCL/4-16 and TRF, but which omits the word *obsessions* on the YSR. We omitted the word *obsessions* from the YSR, because it is unfamiliar and might be confusing to adolescents. Because the item does not explicitly state *obsessions*, the YSR scoring rules also permit counting almost anything an adolescent lists here, except problems that are explicitly listed elsewhere on the YSR. For the CBCL/4-16 and TRF, on the other hand, the scoring instructions exclude anything that is clearly not obsessional. Although the wording and scoring rules do not differ much on items regarded as parallel between the forms, the differences that exist for some items might limit agreement between informants. However, we considered it more important to word and score items appropriately for each type of informant than to strive for identical wording, which might produce more misunderstanding than agreement.

7. What does it mean when a child obtains a problem score in the high clinical range on a form completed by one type of informant but in the low normal range on a form completed by another type of informant?

Answer: When discrepancies of this sort occur between a CBCL and TRF for the same child, it may mean that the child appears to function quite differently at home and school. This is not uncommon, because some children's behavioral/emotional problems may be specific to either the home or school, and not evident in the other context. However, adolescents who obtain high CBCL, TRF, and/or DOF problem scores occasionally report very few problems on the YSR. This is likely to indicate either a lack of awareness of problems or denial that may make the adolescent a poor candidate for talking therapies requiring motivation for change.

8. Why are "profile types" provided only for the CBCL/4-16?

Answer: As described in the CBCL *Manual*, the profile types for the CBCL/4-16 were derived by cluster analyzing profiles of clinically-referred children. These analyses yielded either six or seven clear-cut profile types that classified substantial proportions of referred children of a particular sex/age group. Similar cluster analyses of TRFs and YSRs, however, have not yielded an adequate typology of profile patterns.

References

Achenbach, T. M. (1978). The Child Behavior Profile: I. Boys aged 6-11. *Journal of Consulting and Clinical Psychology, 46*, 478-488.

Achenbach, T. M. (1985). *Assessment and taxonomy of child and adolescent psychopathology.* Newbury Park, CA: Sage.

Achenbach, T. M., & Edelbrock, C. (1981). Behavioral problems and competencies reported by parents of normal and disturbed children aged four to sixteen. *Monographs of the Society for Research in Child Development, 46*, Serial No. 188.

Achenbach, T. M., & Edelbrock, C. (1983). *Manual for the Child Behavior Checklist and Revised Child Behavior Profile.* Burlington, VT: University of Vermont Department of Psychiatry.

Achenbach, T. M., & Edelbrock, C. (1986). *Manual for the Teacher's Report Form and Teacher Version of the Child Behavior Profile.* Burlington, VT: University of Vermont Department of Psychiatry.

Achenbach, T. M., & Edelbrock, C. (1987). *Manual for the Youth Self-Report and Profile.* Burlington, VT: University of Vermont Department of Psychiatry.

Achenbach, T. M., Edelbrock, C., & Howell, C. T. (1987). Empirically-based assessment of the behavioral/emotional problems of 2-3-year-old children. *Journal of Abnormal Child Psychology, 15*, 629-650.

Achenbach, T. M., & McConaughy, S. H. (1987). *Empirically-based assessment of child and adolescent psychopathology: Practical applications.* Newbury Park, CA: Sage.

American Psychiatric Association. (1987). *Diagnostic and statistical manual of mental disorders* (3rd ed. rev.). Washington, D.C.: Author.

Applebaum, S. H. (1970). Science and persuasion in the psychological test report. *Journal of Consulting and Clinical Psychology, 35*, 349-355.

Barkley, R. A. (1987). *Defiant children: A clinician's manual for parent training.* New York: Guilford Press.

Edelbrock, C., & Achenbach, T. M. (1980). A typology of Child Behavior Profile patterns: Distribution and correlates for disturbed children aged 6-16. *Journal of Abnormal Child Psychology, 8,* 441-470.

Edelbrock, C., & Costello, A. J. (1988). Convergence between statistically derived behavior problem syndromes and child psychiatric diagnoses. *Journal of Abnormal Child Psychology,* in press.

Education of the Handicapped Act. Public Law 94-142. (1977). *Federal Register, 42,* p. 42478. Amended in *Federal Register,* (1981), *46,* p. 3866.

Fischer, C. T. (1973). Contextual approach to assessment. *Community Mental Health Journal, 9,* 38-45.

Fischer, C. T. (1979). Individualized assessment and phenomenological psychology. *Journal of Personality Assessment, 43,* 115-122.

Friedlander, S., Weiss, D. S., & Traylor, J. (1986). Assessing the influence of maternal depression on the validity of the Child Behavior Checklist. *Journal of Abnormal Child Psychology, 14,* 123-133.

Goyette, C. H., Conners, C. K., & Ulrich, R. F. (1978). Normative data on revised Conners Parent and Teacher Rating Scales. *Journal of Abnormal Child Psychology, 6,* 221-236.

Kaufman, A. S. (1979). *Intelligent testing with the WISC-R.* New York: Wiley-Interscience.

Kaufman, A. S., & Kaufman, N. L. (1977). *Clinical evaluation of young children with the McCarthy scales.* New York: Grune & Stratton.

Knoff, H. M. (1986). The personality assessment report and the feedback and planning conference. In H. Knoff (Ed.), *The assessment of child and adolescent personality.* New York: Guilford Press.

McConaughy, S. H. (1985). Using the Child Behavior Check-list and related instruments in school-based assessments of children. *School Psychology Review, 14,* 479-494.

McConaughy, S. H., & Achenbach, T. M. (1988). Contribu-tions of developmental psychopathology to school ser-vices. In T. B. Gutkin & C. R. Reynolds (Eds.), *Handbook of school psychology* (2nd ed). New York: Wiley, in press.

McConaughy, S. H., Achenbach, T. M., & Gent, C. L. (1988). Multiaxial empirically based assessment: Parent, teacher, observational, cognitive, and personality corre-lates of Child Behavior Profiles for 6-11-year-old boys. *Journal of Abnormal Child Psychology, 16,* 485-509.

Reed, M., & Edelbrock, C. (1983). Reliability and validity of the Direct Observation Form of the Child Behavior Checklist. *Journal of Abnormal Child Psychology, 11,* 521-530.

Sattler, J. M. (1988). *Assessment of children* (3rd ed.). San Diego: Jerome M. Sattler, Publisher.

INDEX

abuse, sexual, 113, 127, 128
Achenbach, T.M., 1, 2, 4, 6, 12, 18, 36, 45, 54, 71, 118, 127, 129, 133, 134, 139
achievement, school, tests, 4-5, 31, 55, 84-107
adaptive functioning, 40, 45
adolescents, 30-31, 57-70
American Psychiatric Association, 2, 139
Applebaum, S.H., 82, 139
Attention Deficit–Hyperactivity Disorder, 93, 100-101

Barkley, R.A., 96, 140
broad-band scales, 7

case illustrations, 2, 82-128
  CBCL/4-16, 18-26
  CBCL/2-3, 36-38
  TRF, 45-50
  YSR, 62-66
  DOF, 75-79
  forensic, 110-127
  report of, 82-109
child abuse, 30, 113, 127-128
Child Behavior Checklist
  for Ages 4-16 (CBCL/4-16), 12-32, 53
  for Ages 2-3 (CBCL/2-3), 33-39
clinical range, 9
  CBCL/4-16, 21-25, 27
  CBCL/2-3, 37-39
  TRF, 45, 48-51
  YSR, 64-66
  DOF, 79-80

cognitive assessment, 4-5, 87-88, 92, 94, 100, 104-105, 114-115, 121-122
competence, 7, 12, 27-28, 134
computer-scored profile, 18, 21-22, 25-26, 75-76, 78, 116-117, 118-119, 123-125
confidentiality, 53, 69, 102
Conners, C.K., 97, 140
control children (DOF), 74-79
Costello, A.J., 133, 140
cutoff scores,
  CBCL/4-16, 27
  CBCL/2-3, 39
  TRF, 45, 48, 50
  YSR, 64, 66
  DOF, 75, 79-80

diagnosis, 7, 86, 92-93, 97, 99, 100-101, 104, 108-109, 133-134
Diagnostic and Statistical Manual (DSM), 2, 92, 93, 99, 100, 133
direct assessment of child, 4-6, 57-80
Direct Observation Form (DOF), 30, 53, 71-80
disagreements between informants, 90, 93, 126, 127, 128, 131, 137
divorce, 30

Edelbrock, C., 1, 6, 18, 36, 45, 54, 71, 118, 127, 133, 140
empirically-based assessment, 4-11, 128
  forensic reports of, 110-128

142

initiated w. CBCL/4-16, 28-32
initiated w. TRF, 50-56
initiated w. YSR, 67-69
reporting results of, 82-109
Externalizing, 7, 27-28, 135

factor analysis, 7, 12, 33, 45, 57, 74, 135
family assessment, 113, 120-121, 133
Fischer, C.T., 82, 140
follow-up evaluations, 32, 56, 69, 98, 109
forensic reports, 110-128
Friedlander, S., 130, 140

Gent, C.L., 71, 141
Goyette, C.H., 97, 140

hand-scored profile,
CBCL/4-16, 18-25
CBCL/2-3, 36-38
TRF, 45-50
YSR, 62-66
Howell, C.T., 1, 36, 127, 139

Individual Education Plan (IEP), 55, 94, 101, 102, 103, 106
informants, 8
intake information, 28-31
Internalizing, 7, 27-28, 135
interpretations of profiles, 132
interventions, 31, 32, 55, 69, 94-98, 101, 106-109
interviews, 3, 28, 30, 54, 67, 91, 113, 120
intraclass correlation (ICC), 18, 25

Kaufman, A.S., 82, 114, 121, 140
Kaufman, N.L., 114, 121, 140
Knoff, H., 82, 140

McCarthy Scales of Children's Abilities, 114, 121
McConaughy, S.H., 1, 2, 4, 54, 71, 129, 133, 134, 141
Minnesota Child Development Inventory (MCDI), 114-115, 121-122
multiaxial assessment, 4-6, *see also* empirically-based assessment

narrow-band syndrome scales, 7
CBCL/4-16, 12, 17, 27-28
CBCL/2-3, 33-39
TRF, 45-51
YSR, 57, 62-66
DOF, 74-80
normal range, 9
CBCL/4-16, 20, 24, 27
CBCL/2-3, 39
TRF, 45, 50
YSR, 64-66
DOF, 77-79
norms, 8-9, 130
CBCL/4-16, 12
CBCL/2-3, 33
TRF, 45
YSR, 57
DOF, 74

on-task score (DOF), 71-76
Oppositional Defiant Disorder, 92
"other problems" on profiles, 24, 77, 130

parent reports, 4-6, 12-39
Peabody Individual Achievement Test (PIAT), 88, 104-105
pediatricians, 82, 83
percentiles, 8
    CBCL/4-16, 20, 24, 27-28
    CBCL/2-3, 37-39
    TRF, 45-51
    YSR, 64-66
    DOF, 76-79
physical assessment, 4-5
problem scales, 21
    CBCL/4-16, 17, 21-28
    CBCL/2-3, 36-39
    TRF, 45-50
    YSR, 62-66
    DOF, 74-80
profile types, 18, 138
projective assessment, 132-133
Public Law 94-142, 2, 54, 133

reading skills of informants, 90, 132
Reed, M., 71, 141
re-evaluations, 55, 97
reports of findings, 31, 82-128

Sattler, J.M., 82, 87, 141
school psychologists, 50, 54, 67
serious emotional disturbance (SED), 54
sexual behavior, problems, 113, 116-118, 120, 123, 126, 127, 128
social desirability, 130
socially desirable items on YSR, 57
special education, 50, 53, 55, 92, 94, 101, 102, 106, 133

standard scores, 8, 88, 105, see also *T* scores
suicidal behavior, thoughts, 31, 67
syndrome scales, 7, 134, see also narrow-band syndrome scales

T scores (standard scores), 8
    CBCL/4-16, 20, 24, 27-28
    CBCL/2-3, 37-39
    TRF, 48-51
    YSR, 64-66
    DOF, 75-78
Teacher's Report Form (TRF), 4-6, 30, 40-56
tests, 5, 54, 55, 67, 87-107, 114-115, 121-122, 132-133
total problem score,
    CBCL/4-16, 27-28
    CBCL/2-3, 37
    TRF, 45, 48
    YSR, 64
    DOF, 71
training for DOF, 71-74
Traylor, J., 130, 140
Ulrich, R.F., 97, 140

Wechsler Intelligence Scale for Children–Revised (WISC–R), 87, 104
Weiss, D.S., 130, 140

Youth Self-Report (YSR), 30, 53, 57-70